Items should be returned on or before the last date shown below. Items not already requested by other borrowers may be renewed in person, in writing or by telephone. To renew, please quote the number on the barcode label. To renew online a PIN is required. This can be requested at your local library.
Renew online @ **www.dublincitypubliclibraries.ie**
Fines charged for overdue items will include postage incurred in recovery. Damage to or loss of items will be charged to the borrower.

Leabharlanna Poiblí Chathair Bhaile Átha Cliath
Dublin City Public Libraries

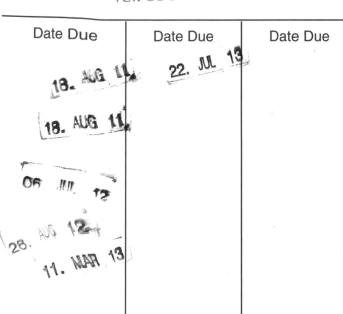

Dublin City
Baile Átha Cliath

Bháile Phib
Phibsboro
Tel: 8304341

Bháile Phib
Phibsboro
Tel: 8304341

sics

Date Due	Date Due	Date Due
18. AUG 11	22. JUL 13	
18. AUG 11		
06 JUL 12		
28. AUG 12		
11. MAR 13		

Flowerdew

An Hachette UK Company
www.hachette.co.uk

A Pyramid Paperback

First published in Great Britain in 2007 by
Hamlyn, a division of Octopus Publishing Group Ltd
2–4 Heron Quays, London E14 4JP
www.octopusbooks.co.uk
www.octopusbooksusa.com

This edition published in 2008
Copyright © Octopus Publishing Group Limited
2007, 2008

Distributed in the U.S. and Canada by
Octopus Books USA:
c/o Hachette Book Group USA
237 Park Avenue
New York NY 10017

This material was previously published as *Go Organic!*

ISBN 978-0-600-61909-3

A CIP catalogue record for this book
is available from the British Library

Printed and bound in China

10 9 8 7 6 5 4 3 2

Left: Edible chrysanthemums and dill.

Right: The coneflower (Rudbeckia hirta).

Contents

Introduction

Concerns about the pesticides, fungicides, insecticides and other chemical sprays used in what is generally called 'conventional' gardening and food production have made more and more of us question what it is, exactly, that we eat. When these anxieties are combined with an increased awareness of the damage, possibly irreparable, that we are doing to the environment, it is not surprising that many people nowadays are actively adopting organic principles in their gardens. If you grow your own vegetables, fruit and herbs in an organic garden you know that they are free from the slightest taint of chemicals and that in growing them you have done nothing to harm the environment.

The aim of the organic gardener is to create an environment in which healthy plants can be grown successfully and pests and diseases discouraged without damaging or polluting the soil or destroying wildlife. Nature has created its own system of checks and balances, predators and prey, and if you create an environment in which they all flourish side by side, then nature will do much of the work for you.

The organic approach has been developed in response to the damage caused by conventional methods. Gardening (like commercial farming) has long been practised as a form of warfare, in which crops are grown by doing battle with pests and diseases and by artificially stimulating their soil. Bad soil management, profligate use of chemicals and overcropping have resulted in desertification and loss of productive land throughout the world and we are doing the same to our gardens.

Organic principles

Protecting and increasing life in the soil is the first and most important principle of organic gardening. We are dependent on a healthy topsoil to feed us: if it becomes overworked it will erode and blow away, as has already happened on some overworked and overfarmed land. The only way to maintain, improve and increase topsoil is by actively encouraging the multitude of micro-organisms in the soil so that they can convert minerals and organic material into nutrients available for plant growth. It is these by-products that build up water-retentive, loamy, humus-rich soil – the soil that promotes healthy plants. In return for short-term gains, using chemical fertilizers and overcropping burn off this store of nutrients and destroy the organisms.

Organic gardening works by feeding the soil, not the plants, and by using organic material instead of soluble chemicals. The burgeoning life in the soil uses this organic material, minerals and the greater amounts of retained water to produce more life. Plants then feed on the by-products, taking what they need to make their own growth.

The effect of adding organic material is cumulative: as more is introduced it encourages populations of soil flora and fauna. These larger populations support yet more life forms. So the variety and quantity of by-products increases, raising the fertility of the soil. The plants living off this balanced diet are more healthy and resistant to pests and diseases than those living in denatured soil pumped up with cocktails of chemical fertilizers and kept going with poisonous sprays. To protect the life in the soil, organic gardeners use no poisonous substances that can harm them, apart from 'natural' ones in the last resort. These are deemed to be acceptable because they are less wide-ranging in their toxicity and break down rapidly and naturally after use.

Animals in the garden

The increasing life in an organic soil then goes on to support more and larger forms of life in the garden and surrounding environment. After all, if you want blackbirds then you have to have worms. Again, the effects are cumulative. As more and larger forms of life come to the table of your soil they bring in minerals and nutrients, further enhancing its fertility. For example, birds shed feathers, eggshells, nesting material, copious droppings and eventually their bodies, all of which contribute to the soil's fertility as they are broken down and reabsorbed into the chain of life.

Other creatures, such as frogs, toads and hedgehogs, take part in the same process, and all give off carbon dioxide, which is rapidly reabsorbed by garden plants. Few people realize how important this gas is for plant growth or that growing plants can extract all of it from still air in only minutes of bright sunlight. Animal life of any size in or on the soil gives off carbon dioxide and thus maintains growth.

Organic gardening also aims to mimic nature by increasing plant cover. In nature, bare soil soon disappears under a tangle of weeds and brambles, and in time tree and shrub seedlings turn it into dense woodland. All this growth increases the soil underneath while it fixes sunlight and extracts

Above: The tayberry is a delicious new loganberry variety with larger, sweeter fruits.

more carbon dioxide from the air. Organic gardeners interplant between crops and use green manures before and after planting. These methods produce a natural soil cover that ensures soil stability, prevents wind and water erosion and builds up the soil over time. The increased mixture and variety of plants not only aids pest and disease control but also improves the local ecology, providing a mini conservation area from which beneficial wildlife can move out to recolonize the local countryside.

The organic system further benefits the environment because it is far more self-sustaining, requiring less input. Home-grown fertility from green manures and compost replaces bought-in chemical fertilizers, and with subtler pest and disease control there is no need for direct intervention with ecologically damaging agrochemical pesticides.

Achieving an organic garden, improving your soil, recycling natural materials, avoiding chemicals, growing a wide range of plants and attracting wildlife are all very simple, as this book proves.

Step 1

Improve your soil

Few people get the opportunity to choose the site or the soil for their gardens, and most of us have to make the best of what we've got. Many gardens are on old sites, which may be exhausted and pest-ridden. Some gardens are likely to be polluted and out of balance, especially if many chemicals have been used. On the other hand, abandoned or derelict sites, full of rampant weeds, will (unlikely as it seems) probably have good soil.

Understanding your soil

Most soils will produce flowers, shrubs or tree fruit without much improvement, but they will need more attention if you want to grow vegetables. Problem soils tend to be common to a particular locality, and it is always a good idea to see how your neighbours cope. Almost all soils can be easily improved, but it may be worth putting on extra topsoil if it is poor or polluted.

Most types of soil need the same basic treatment to improve them – that is, the addition of copious quantities of organic material. Anything else is almost inconsequential by comparison. However, although most soils can be improved and thus made acceptable to a wider range of plants, there is a difference between improvement and change. It is hard to change the basic soil type, which determines what you can grow well, and it will make life easier if you accept what you've got rather than trying to modify it drastically. For example, trying to make a lime soil suitable for rhododendrons is futile; it is far better to grow philadelphus, fuchsias, cotoneasters and other lime-lovers.

Acidity and alkalinity

It is worth testing the acidity or alkalinity (lime content) of the soil, but do not use cheap meters, which are inaccurate. Simple chemical test kits with an accurate colour chart are available in most garden shops. The basic pH may vary at ground level and further down if the soil layers have built up a rich surface mould, so take a number of samples from a typical worked soil. The pH may change as the soil is enriched, particularly as more organic material is added. This tends to make soils more acid.

Adding lime to the soil every few years will be of benefit in most gardens, especially for vegetables and grassed areas. (Check if it is needed, though, because over-liming can cause its own problems.) Lime can take the form of chalk or, better, dolomitic lime, which contains more magnesium and other nutrients. Best of all is calcified seaweed, which contains all the trace elements as well as lime, although it can be rather slow-acting.

Never mix lime with manure or compost. Apply it before rain is expected on top of the soil or grass, and rake, brush or allow it to leach in. Late winter is generally the best time. In a vegetable rotation it is probably best applied before peas or brassicas, but not before potatoes.

If, on the other hand, your soil has a lot of chalk, it may be lacking in available trace elements. To improve the soil you will need to use raised beds (see page 83) and dig in plenty of manure or compost.

Adding improvers

Various materials are offered as soil improvers. Some flocculating agents based on lime or gypsum do help clay soils to form lighter textures, but most soils will benefit more from extra organic material, though sharp sand and grit will also help open up a heavy soil.

Soil analysis

Analysis is unnecessary for most gardens, and you will get better value from a bag of seaweed meal. It is difficult to get accurate readings from the patchy soils in gardens, which can contain all sorts of detritus. If you aim to incorporate some broad-spectrum organic fertilizers and as much organic material as possible, most soils will balance themselves.

A more useful guide is to look at the plants that are growing well. For example, if your neighbours' gardens are full of flourishing rhododendrons, azaleas and heathers, grow these plants too because the soil is obviously suitable, whatever the analysis says. Good gardeners grow what does well rather than coaxing unsuitable plants to grow in the wrong places.

Above: Rhododendrons need an acid soil to thrive, so if they grow in your garden you have acid soil.

Soil types

All soils contain the same materials – stones, silt, sands, clays and organic matter – but in varying proportions. What affects plants most is not the nutrient levels of the soil but its physical texture, aeration and moisture retention. All (except peaty soils) will be improved considerably by adding more organic material, especially when it is combined with a mulch (see page 54).

Adding organic material contributes directly to the nutrient level and helps to increase another component of healthy soil: micro-organisms. Mainly fungi, bacteria and other microbes, these break down organic material to release further nutrients. These resources are then made available to the plants. In most soils, there is sufficient of almost every element to last for millions of years of heavy cropping – if micro-organisms have the materials and conditions to thrive.

> Worms are probably the most important creatures in the garden

Air and water

First of all, micro-organisms need water, the most important factor for encouraging all life. Air is the next most important component. Almost all microlife and plant roots need oxygen and give off carbon dioxide. Much of the carbon dioxide is reabsorbed by the soil, but fresh air is needed to restore the oxygen content. Organic particles keep soils open and allow aeration.

Soil composition

Soil composition varies with depth. Only the top few centimetres (an inch or so) throb with life, and this layer constitutes the most productive part of the soil. Keep it at its best by regularly adding an organic mulch to keep the soil warm, fed and moist. At depths of more than 30cm (12in), in the subsoil, only worms and plant roots live. The working depth of 'living' soil is most efficiently maintained by their action alone: it is rarely practicable to dig to their depths. Digging may sometimes be necessary, but it disrupts the soil layers and should never bring up sterile subsoil.

Encouraging worms

Worms are vital. Their casts have a granular texture which promotes root growth and their burrows act as aeration and drainage channels. The digestive process of worms reduces mineral particles in size, making them more accessible to micro-organisms.

Encourage worms by keeping the soil moist and covered with a mulch. Feed bare soil and mulched areas with a handful of grass clippings every month or so as worms need 'greens' as well as organic material, such as compost or well-rotted manure. Ground seaweed, blood, fish and bone meal and hoof and horn meal will also feed them. Rotary cultivating the soil will kill worms.

Know your soil

	Advantages	Disadvantages	Treatment
Heavy clay	• Rich soil • Rarely suffers from mineral deficiencies • Resists drought well • Good for fixed-bed gardening • Excellent for cauliflowers	• Hard to dig • Sticks to everything • Sets almost solid in dry weather • Drains poorly and pools with water in heavy rain • Encourages slugs	• Never allow to compact while wet • Add coarse organic material and sharp sand or grit • Will benefit from liming
Light, sandy soil	• Easy to dig • Washes off tools and shoes • Never pools with water • Warms earlier • Excellent for carrots if not too stony	• Loses humus quickly • Nutrients wash out easily • Dries out badly	• Add plenty of organic material, rock dusts (especially ground rock potash) and organic fertilizers
Silt	• Fairly easily to dig • Good for most crops if well nourished	• Does not retain water • Tends to splash and cap badly in wet weather	• Add ground rock dusts
Peat	• High in organic material • Excellent for salad crops and soft fruits • Suits calcifuge plants (e.g. azaleas, some heathers)	• Sometimes short of nutrients • Dries out easily • Not stable enough for large trees • Good soil for weeds	• Add lime to broaden range of plants that can be grown
Loam	• Produced when old meadow or grass sward is dug up • Best because it encourages production of fine root hairs	• Hard to find • Possession encourages complacency	• Will need some annual organic material to maintain its fertility
Wet soil	• Although not suited to most crops, can be used to create magnificient ornamental gardens • Ideal for blueberries and cranberries	• Tends to be sour or acid	• Add large amounts of organic material to improve drainage and water dispersion • Add lime if necessary • Drain if low-lying
Lime or chalky soil	• Good for brassicas if also rich and moist • Good for many trees, figs and grapes	• Causes chlorosis in calcifuge plants by locking up iron and other nutrients	• Add organic material and mulch plants for best results
Stony soil	• Tends to be free-draining • Best for permanent plantings rather than annuals and vegetables	• Difficult to hoe and cultivate	• Add thin layer of sharp sand to create workable tilth

Drainage and digging

The aim of the organic gardener is to give plants the best conditions possible and to prevent them from ever coming under stress. Protection is needed from extremes of heat and cold and, most importantly, from water stress, which is most effectively achieved by increasing the organic matter and thus the humus content of the soil, which acts like a sponge, retaining moisture. However, too much water can be as bad as too little, so take care to get the balance right.

Drainage

Waterlogging kills plants by driving out air. It is more of a problem on heavy soils, because the finer particles hold much more water than the coarse grains of sand or silt. It may be necessary to install a drainage system in the worst cases, but often breaking up compacted soil, encouraging earthworms with lime and mulches, applying organic material and using raised beds will help the soil absorb the water, rather than just allowing it to drain away. If drainage is needed, ditches may work, or you may need to lay herringbones of drainage pipes leading to a soakaway.

> Many gardens are run successfully without ever being dug

Clay soils retain more water than sandy, chalky or stony ones, which all need much more watering in dry regions. It is the humus part of the soil that soaks up water, and so the higher the organic content the more water can be retained. Keep the soil moist, hoe the surface or mulch and trap evaporation with layer upon layer of plants.

Dig or no-dig

There has been much controversy over no-dig and digging methods, and both sides are partly right. The greater part of most gardens is no-dig anyway, and it is only the vegetable plot that gets dug regularly.

Certainly, digging a new plot is a good idea, if only to unearth and remove rubbish and roots, but as an annual event it appears to be unproductive. The effort would be better spent on turning the compost heap or weeding, as any increase in yield

Breaking new ground

At some time most of us want to make a new bed where none was before. The most important aspect is to remove all of the established weeds. Before embarking on the actual task it is a good idea to check that there are no pipes or wires under the ground and to dig carefully, as they may not be buried deep enough. Without doubt the easiest way to start a new bed is to put the whole area down to closely cut grass for a year or two and to cut the bed out of the sward. It helps to be patient and plan ahead.

from digging is less than that obtained from one good watering at the right time for most crops.

Digging annually breaks up the natural soil layers, the network of earthworm tunnels and decaying root systems. It aerates the soil, causing excessive humus breakdown with a short-term increase in fertility, which may leach out if the digging precedes the crop by a long time. The need to produce a good seedbed does not justify digging unless the soil has been badly compacted; mulching and surface cultivation will make just as good a tilth. However, most soils show benefit from a thorough digging once every five to ten years; if nothing else, this does destroy mole runs and ants' nests and the like. Many gardens are run successfully without ever being dug.

Digging benefits heavy soils more than lighter ones as frost may then help to break them down into a good crumb structure, but if badly dug it can just make clods and air gaps. Light soil, which is easy to dig, needs it least.

No-dig methods mostly include permanent paths and fixed or raised beds so that the soil is not compacted by traffic. See also pages 82–3.

Above: 'Early Onward' peas grown with sweetcorn and potatoes. Arranging plants close together helps to retain moisture in the soil.

Digging dos and don'ts

Do	Don't
✓ Pace yourself	✗ Work for too long
✓ Break each lump	✗ Dig sodden soil
✓ Mix in well-rotted manure as you go	✗ Try to move too large a spit
✓ Dig heavy soils in drier autumn weather	
✓ Leave lighter soils until late winter so nutrients don't leach out	

Soil fertility

You get better results with almost any plant from a deep, rich, moist soil full of organic material, so every effort should be made to improve the soil before planting. Needless to say, it will be much more difficult later on. All poor sites will need building up with copious quantities of organic material before you can even think about planting.

Maintaining soil fertility

In general, if you regularly feed your soil with well-rotted manure and compost, it will remain fertile. In addition, the rotation of crops on the vegetable plot leaves root and leaf residues, and this will be increased if green manures are grown between crops and then hoed or dug in (see pages 18–20). Regular feeding of the plants as such does not take place in an organic system, but the soil is fed with plant residues as well as compost or well-rotted farmyard manure mixed in whenever a heavy feeder or perennial is planted.

> Environmentally concerned gardeners will avoid using peat extracted from peat bogs

Mulches of organic material break down and are soon incorporated. Rock dusts, especially potash, can be added with benefit at any time, but take several seasons to act. Ground rock dusts provide additional raw materials of the most needed elements in a finely distributed form and benefit most soils, especially lighter ones. For poor soils in the first few years, some supplementary feeding may be undertaken with organic fertilizers of a faster-acting nature. These are crutches, and should be discarded as the soil becomes enriched. Far more important for fertility is ensuring that the life in the soil is active; mulching and keeping the soil moist helps most.

Peat

Peat is partly decomposed plant material that accumulates in bogs at a very slow rate, so it is theoretically a sustainable resource. But it is currently extracted on a profligate industrial scale from irreplaceable sites of scientific and wildlife significance. Environmentally concerned gardeners will avoid using peat extracted from bogs, though that from reservoir bottoms may be acceptable. In any case peat makes a poor mulch as it is too fine; much better alternatives are composted manures or bark, mushroom, cocoa and coir wastes (see page 57).

Peat also has very little fertility value and it is really best reserved for specialist potting composts, especially for ericaceous (effectively meaning 'peat-loving') plants. In most other potting composts peat is not as desirable as leafmould or good loam. Soil-less (loam-free) composts are popular as they are light and easy to use but the peat they contain most often comes from non-renewable sources. There are now many good, alternative growing mediums, including those based on coir, bark, crop residues and even, in some areas, composted council waste.

Peat-free sowing and potting compost ingredients

Ingredient	Advantages	Disadvantages
Coir	• Widely available • Effective • Free of weed seeds	• Easy to water badly
Composted bark	• Effective • Free of weed seeds • Good ecologically	• Easy to water badly
Composted crop wastes	• Effective • Free of weed seeds • Good ecologically	• Easy to water badly • Potential residues
Leafmould	• Superb • Roots love it	• Not free of wed seeds • Hard to get good quality in quantity
Loam (rotted down grass turves)	• Effective • Heavy • Roots love it	• Not free of wed seeds • Hard to buy good quality
Sieved garden compost	• Effective • Heavy • Rich in nutrients	Full of weed seeds Impossible to buy
Well–rotted manure	• Effective • Available in quantity • Rich in nutrients	• Not free of disease or weed-seeds • Easy to water badly • Potential residues
Composted municipal wastes	• Effective • Available in quantity • Some nutrients	• Potentially full of residues
Sharp sand and grit	• Widely available • Cheap • Superb drainage	• No nutrient- or water-holding value • Needs mixing with others

Fertilizers, liquid feeds and manures

Fertilizers

Conventional fertilizers are ranked according to the relative proportions of nitrogen, phosphorus and potassium they contain. They are regarded as direct plant foods, replacing the elements taken away with the crops. Nitrogen (N) is considered to stimulate leafy growth, phosphorus (P) to feed roots, and potassium (K) to promote fruiting and increase disease resistance. These elements exist naturally in the soil, but it is not natural to have them in high concentrations, as occurs when they are applied as soluble fertilizers.

Organic gardeners protect the micro-organisms in the soil by avoiding substances that can damage them; instead, they use fertilizers that are effectively insoluble so they cannot become too concentrated in the soil solution. These fertilizers need to be broken down and incorporated by micro-organisms before they can increase the nutrient supply in the soil and become available to plants. Thus they do not leach out as readily, and remain beneficial for longer.

> Organic gardeners protect the micro-organisms in the soil by avoiding substances that can damage them

Organic fertilizers may, therefore, be considered more as soil stimulators than as plant fertilizers as they promote increases in soil life, and the by-products from this increased population then feed the plants. Because they are stimulators or catalysts, they do not need to be applied in large quantities. A handful per square metre (yard) every other year is usually sufficient.

Note that blood, fish and bone meal, bone meal and hoof and horn are ethically dubious, and likely to be taken by animals or birds unless they are mixed in well with the soil; keep the bags in a safe place.

Seaweed meal

This contains a wide spread of trace elements and 2–3 per cent each of nitrogen and potassium, but only a sixth as much phosphate. The most widely acceptable nitrogenous fertilizer and soil stimulator, seaweed meal is also a good compost activator.

It is more pleasant to use and more acceptable ecologically than blood, fish and bone meal for a general-purpose feed. It is expensive but long-lasting, and it is better balanced when mixed with bone meal or ground rock phosphate, but is effective enough on its own for most plants. It should be raked into the soil in spring.

Blood, fish and bone meal

This traditional, organically based fertilizer is both effective and fast-acting, and should be used in moderation. Rake it in immediately before planting hungry feeders or mix it with the planting soil. Beware of cheap brands, however, which are frequently adulterated with chemical fertilizers and sand.

Bone meal

An excellent source of phosphates, bone meal acts most quickly in fine soil. Although expensive, it is good for incorporating in the soil when planting, particularly woody plants and strawberries.

Hoof and horn

Although expensive, hoof and horn is an effective slow-release source of nitrogen for hungry and woody plants.

Calcified seaweed

This fertilizer is more of a lime than a fertilizer, but because of its high level of trace elements it may act like a fertilizer by stimulating soil life. It is considerably cheaper than seaweed and may, therefore, be used as a general-purpose fertilizer where the lime will be no disadvantage. Calcified seaweed is especially beneficial for turf, brassicas, legumes and stone fruits.

Ground rock potash

This is exactly what its name suggests: a ground rock dust. It releases potash slowly and is best used by being mixed in composts or into the soil at any time every two or three years, particularly

Above: 'Cambridge Vigour' strawberries in midsummer ready for picking. Strawberries benefit from having bone meal incorporated into the soil at planting time.

Above: Runner beans, like all leguminous plants, will benefit from an application of calcified seaweed, which contains high levels of trace elements.

on light soils and in wet areas. It is especially good for gooseberries and culinary apples and for promoting disease resistance in plants.

Ground rock phosphate

This rock dust is useful for restoring healthy life to abused or over-acid soils, especially in wet areas. Mix it in composts or in the soil at any time. It is especially good for strawberries.

Ground rock basalt or granite

This finely ground rock dust, which may also be added to any soil, contains a spread of minerals to encourage micro-organisms and is claimed to revitalize worn-out soils.

Wood ash

Wood ashes are a rich source of potash, but it is in a soluble form which leaches out of the soil. The ash should, therefore, be applied to growing crops, especially fruit and onions, for ripening and disease protection. Sprinkle on the surface and rake in or add to the compost heap.

Commercial balanced 'organic' fertilizers

These commercial preparations are usually expensive. Most are based on animal wastes, which have been composted or worm composted. They may be contaminated with diseases and residues, so only those with the Soil Association or similar symbol can be recommended.

Sewage sludge

Because this, too, is likely to be contaminated, it can be recommended only for ornamental plantings where it is a slow-release source of phosphate. Avoid using in vegetable gardens.

Liquid feeds

Plants confined in containers are restricted and cannot reach farther afield for nutrients after they have used up those around the rootball. They need feeding little and often with a liquid feed diluted in their water. These liquid feeds may smell unpleasant, but this disappears when they are absorbed into the soil. All the feeds discussed below are for plants with restricted root runs, though they may be used in moderation on hungry plants in the open such as sweetcorn.

Comfrey liquid

Comfrey leaves are collected, packed into a container (such as a water butt), activated with a little urine and covered in water. They rot down in four to five weeks to form a solution like black tea. It smells horrible, but watered down to a pale straw colour is a perfectly balanced feed for tomatoes and other plants. Another method is to stack the leaves in a covered container with a hole in the base, and leave them to rot down without added liquid. After a few weeks a liquid concentrate will start to drip out. This again can be diluted and used as a liquid feed. The concentrate can also be used as the fertility constituent in potting mixes.

Nettle tea

This is made and used in the same way as comfrey liquid, using nettles instead. As well as being a good balanced feed, it is claimed to make plants more resistant to diseases and pests. Similarly, bags of manure can be hung in sacks in water butts and the resulting solution used in the same way as nettle tea.

Seaweed solution

Diluted down and used as a beneficial liquid feed, this carries the benefits of a wider range of trace elements, but is expensive to use for general watering and should be saved for use as a foliar feed. The effect on plants is rapid and marked. They take on a darker, healthier colour and resist pests and diseases better.

Fish emulsion

A rich source of nutrients, this is especially effective when it is mixed with seaweed solution and applied as a liquid feed.

Animal manures

Manure is probably the best soil improver of all, but you have to take what you can get and that from intensive rearing units may contain unacceptable residues. All animal manures make a contribution to soil fertility, but they should always be well composted before use. This will help to get rid of some chemical contaminants. Avoid manures from farms that use intensive rearing methods as there will be contaminants from the feed or from drugs or hormones administered to the animals – pig and poultry manure from intensive farms should be particularly avoided. The straw or wood shavings the manures come in may themselves be polluted.

> One barrow-load of
> manure will muck
> 10 square metres
> (12 square yards)

Above: Comfrey liquid is a cheap and effective liquid feed which can be made at home using comfrey leaves. Nettle tea is made in the same way.

Stack the manure in a heap, cover it to protect it from the rain, and leave for a year if possible. As a rule, one barrow-load of manure will muck 10 square metres (12 square yards).

In order of preference, horse, sheep and goat manures are all sweet to handle; cow manure is less pleasant; pig manure is vile and often contains unacceptable contaminants. Rabbit and pet droppings can be added to the compost heap, but cat and dog tray litter is best buried under trees. Poultry manures are strong, highly nitrogenous and a good source of potash. They make a compost heap cook! Never put raw poultry droppings on plants; always compost them first.

Mushroom compost

Non-organic mushroom compost should be avoided as it is also likely to be contaminated with persistent and undesirable chemicals.

Green manures

Any plants that are grown as temporary groundcover and are then dug into the soil as fertilizer are known as green manures, although in some cases the tops of the plants may be cut and composted for use elsewhere. They are usually grown over winter when the soil is vacant, but may also be grown between crops and incorporated as seedlings after only a week or two. They prevent soil erosion and leaching and convert otherwise wasted winter sunlight into useful organic plant matter.

Any plants that grow over winter will do, but those that are easiest to incorporate or that create most bulk are best. Leguminous plants,

Green manures

Manure	Advantages	Disadvantages
Alfalfa (lucerne)	• Deep-rooting and pulls up minerals from 6m (20ft)	• Slow-growing • For nitrogen-fixing, soil must be treated with *Rhizobium* bacteria (sold with seed)
Beans and peas	• Any variety suitable, but only hardy ones will overwinter	• Crop rotation is important when used in vegetable plot
Buckwheat	• Grows quickly in late spring/early summer • Can be left to flower as it is good for beneficial insects • Deep roots and will choke out most weeds	• Not nitrogen-fixing • Must be removed before it sets seed
Clover	• Rich source of nitrogen • Good for bees if allowed to flower	• Needs a year or so to show full benefit • Inclined to regrow
Chicory		• Long-term plant, best used in grass and clover leys as it has deep taproots that take time to form (and kill)
Fenugreek	• Nitrogen-fixing • Quick-growing and suitable for use after early crops or between others • Unrelated to vegetables and so no problem with rotation • Can be sown late spring to late summer but is killed by first frosts	

Green manures

Manure	Advantages	Disadvantages
Fodder radish	• Killed by hard frosts, leaving considerable bulk, which can be easily incorporated into the soil in spring	• Related to brassicas so must be used sparingly in rotations including these crops • Hard to dig in
Hungarian grazing rye	• Sow from late summer to mid-autumn for quick groundcover for overwintering	• Not nitrogen fixing • Very hard to dig in and this must be done a month before the crop to allow time for rotting
Limnanthes douglasii	• Good for producing bulk and suppressing weeds • Sown late summer or autumn it will overwinter • Good for beneficial insects if left	• No drawbacks
Lupins	• Nitrogen-fixing • Deep-rooted • Sown in spring and incorporated in autumn, will help to improve sour, acid land	• Agricultural forms are better than ordinary garden lupins
Mustard	• Fast-growing • When incorporated as seedlings can reduce many infestations of the soil • Best grown between crops or up until the frosts and incorporated *in situ*	• Not nitrogen-fixing • In the brassica family and must be grown with care in rotations; ideally only to the seedling stage • Will not withstand hard winters
Phacelia tanacetifolia	• Attracts bees and hoverflies • Sown in early spring to early autumn, it may overwinter • Easy to remove from the soil or to incorporate in it	• Not nitrogen fixing • Seed is expensive (but can be saved)
Trefoil	• A nitrogen-fixing legume, similar to clover and related to alfalfa • Tolerates shade so can be grown beneath taller crops • Sow from early spring to late autumn and will overwinter	• Prefers alkaline soil
Valerianella (corn salad)	• Good for producing bulk and suppressing weeds • Sow late summer or autumn for overwintering • Edible	• No drawbacks
Winter tares	• Good for producing bulk and suppressing weeds • Nitrogen-fixing • Can be sown from early spring to late autumn for overwintering	• Hard to dig in

Above: Buckwheat is an excellent, fast-growing green manure. Remove or dig in the plants before they can set seed.

Above: Limnanthes douglasii is a good choice as a green manure as it both suppresses weeds and creates bulk.

which fix nitrogen, are frequently used because this nutrient is always in short supply. The manures are usually sown as soon as the ground is bare and until the first frosts start. Those surviving over winter are killed off by impenetrable mulches or are dug in before the crops need the soil. Several weeks of breakdown are necessary for some of the more fibrous green

> Never let green manures flower and go to seed

manures, such as grazing rye, but less time is needed for younger and more succulent growth.

Never let green manures flower and go to seed or the goodness will be lost from the plants. In general, too, it is better to grow two or three short crops than one long-lasting one.

Peas and beans are removed minus their roots before they form pods, leaving nitrogen-rich nodules in the soil. 'Banner' is a hardy variety of broad (field) bean, which is often grown as a green manure. 'Alsike' is the best clover for poor, wet or acid soils, while white clover is better on lighter and limier soils. 'Essex Red' is considered the best clover for green manuring, although it is not reliably hardy and does better on loamy soils.

Minerals

Some garden plants and many weeds are particularly good at accumulating large amounts of minerals and trace elements. In fact, these plants often abound on deficient soils because they are the most successful at grabbing scarce resources. Nettles, for example, indicate that the soil is rich in phosphorus, but clover grows best on soil that is deficient in nitrogen. Although these plants extract most of the nutrients, more will be dissolved into the soil from otherwise insoluble mineral sources. Growing these plants as green manures removes scarce minerals, but once they are composted the concentrated material can be put back to boost the soil. Remember that only annual weeds should be used as green manure as perennial weeds are hard to eradicate.

Mineral accumulators

Mineral	Benefits	Source
Calcium	Promotes development of plant cell walls	Concentrated by buckwheat, *Matricaria recutita* (corn camomile), corn marigold, dandelion, fat hen, goosegrass, melons, purslane and shepherd's purse
Nitrogen	Promotes healthy foliage	Taken from the air (not the soil) and best accumulated with leguminous plants and by digging in any succulent seedlings in their first flushes of growth
Phosphorus	Promotes healthy root development	Concentrated by fat hen, corn marigold, purslane, vetches and the weed *Datura stramonium* (thornapple)
Potassium	Promotes formation of flowers and fruit	Accumulated by several plants, including chickweed, chicory, fat hen, goosegrass, plantain, purslane, thornapple, sweet tobaccos and vetches
Silica	Promotes disease resistance	Made active by plantains, couchgrass, stinging nettles and horsetails (*Equisetum*)
Sulphur	Promotes disease resistance	Accumulates in *Allium* (onion family), brassicas, fat hen and purslane

Step 2 Make your own compost

Making your own compost brings a number of benefits: it avoids wastage, is cost-efficient and gives you the confidence that no unwanted chemicals, pests or diseases are present. As long as you bear in mind a few simple rules, it is not difficult and can be immensely satisfying.

About compost

Composting is the accelerated rotting-down of once-living things. It converts waste into a brown, soil-like mass that is pleasant to smell and use. This mass is almost pure plant food and is in a form readily available to plant roots with no risk of the overfeeding or imbalance that can be caused by chemical fertilizers. Moreover, the vast number of different micro-organisms that have broken down the compost go on to colonize the soil once the compost is added, further aiding fertility.

> Sievings from previous compost heaps are the best activator of all

All manures and other organic materials for use in the garden are better composted before use, except clean commercial mulching materials and clean straw. Fresh manures contain soluble nutrients, which can be too strong for healthy growth, but if they are stacked and turned they compost. Once composted, their fertility is less easily lost and they become safer for plant roots. This is why it is always recommended that only well-rotted farmyard manure is used. Because of the variety of materials going into a compost heap, garden compost contains a greater spread of nutrients and more varied microlife than well-rotted manure, so it is used in preference.

As the composting process converts most of the nutrients into an insoluble form there is little danger of their washing out into the water table in heavy rainfall. However, they do leach out slowly, so compost heaps and rotting manures should always be covered.

Troubleshooting

Problem	Action
Too wet	Remake with extra straw or dry material
Too dry	Add water, fresh wet manure or grass clippings to the heap
Dry with white coating on material	Add water mixed with urine to add liquid and nitrogen

Making compost

There are many different ways of composting, but they all come back to one principle.

• In general, composting proceeds best when there are many, varied materials, well divided, moistened and thoroughly mixed together with plentiful air.

When to use compost

Fresh compost, even when immature, can be mixed into the soil when you are planting trees and shrubs, but if it is to be used as a top dressing or with small plants, such as when planting out cabbages, it is best used matured and sieved. This takes extra effort but produces a finer material, and the residue can then be used to start the next heap. In any case, compost or well-rotted manure is best applied to growing crops in early spring, so that the nutrients are taken up rather than leaching out of the soil over the winter months.

• It helps to have roughly equal amounts of dry material and fresh green material as too much of either will cause poor composting.

• Adding water when mixing is usually necessary as many materials are too dry on their own.

• An activator is not essential, but speeds things up if added during the mixing. Rather than chemical additives it is better to use urine or poultry manure. Seaweed or blood, fish and bone meal will do instead. Sievings from previous compost heaps are the best activator of all, and, if you are starting your first heap, try to get some from a more experienced gardener to mix in.

Covering the heap

Keeping the rain out and the heat in the heap is usually best done with a plastic sheet or two and some insulation such as bubble plastic or carpet laid over the heap. The sides of the heap should also be insulated in cold weather, but they are best made open to allow air in and out as the heap matures. The top of the compost heap must stay covered to dry the heap out ready for sieving and to prevent some of the nutrients leaching out.

Above: Wooden compost containers allow the air to circulate around all sides of the heap. Many, like this one, have removable slats at the front for easy access.

slimy, mix in some torn-up paper or unglazed cardboard. Having a bin on a stand makes turning out potentially easier but filling harder work. Rotary composters only work well with soft materials.

How long?

If insulated and mixed well with only soft and green materials, a heap can be ready in less than a month in summer. If made by slow accumulation in layers in a badly insulated bin, then it will take about three years.

To turn or not

It is always better to turn and re-mix the compost heap; the more the better, especially if the heap is small. Extra grass clippings, urine and dung can be added at this stage to make it cook properly if it is poor stuff. If the compost appears to be wet and

Maturing the heap

I like to plunge a crowbar down into the centre of my heap once it is going. It has little effect, but I love to pull it out and watch it steam, showing me the heap is cooking well. Once the heap has been turned and cooked at least twice it is left to mature for six months, when it is ready for use. If you leave it longer, the worms mineralize it, increasing its richness but decreasing the quantity. It makes excellent potting compost, albeit containing some weed seeds.

Small composters

	Advantages	Disadvantages
Plastic	Often free or subsidized Easy to assemble and use	Usually too small and poorly insulated Ecologically dubious Aesthetically grim
Wood	More aesthetic Easy to make at home	Expensive, as it will rot in a few years Too small and too poorly insulated

Compost containers

Several different styles of compost containers are sold, but most are on the small side and thus do not heat up enough to make really good compost unless given extra insulation.

Simple constructions of wood, wire netting or brick, about 1m (3ft) in height, width and depth are sufficient, and considerably cheaper. I prefer to use four old pallets tied at the corners. These are easily obtained. Do not paint the compost bin with creosote as this will slow the process. A lid will keep out the rain, but an old carpet and a plastic sheet will be better for retaining the heat and will prevent a flush of weeds from growing on top.

In a small garden

In a small garden a compost bin or a container is more suitable than a straggly, untidy heap of the kind that can be tucked away at the bottom of a largish garden. Make your own container from a square cage of wire netting supported by four stout posts driven into the ground. Ideally, make the front removable so that you can easily get to the rotted compost inside.

Traditional bins made from slatted wood will keep the compost looking tidy. They can be easily made from second-hand wooden pallets or planks, or you can buy wood cut to length that slots neatly together. Some of the better composters are supplied with wooden tops; otherwise, remember to cover the full bin with old carpet and plastic to keep in the heat and stop the rain getting into the compost.

Cone-shaped, black or dark green plastic composters, which hold from 220 to 300 litres (8–10 cu ft) or more, are a tidy and convenient alternative to a heap. In a small garden the problem is often that there is insufficient waste material to allow a sufficiently large heap to build up, so the material never gets hot enough to begin to break down. You will get far better results with two smallish bins: fill one and leave it for a time or, better, mix and turn it into the second, additionally insulated, heap to cook and mature while you begin to fill up the first bin again.

> Do not paint the bin with creosote as this will slow the composting

Instant containers

Convert a dead fridge or small freezer into a hot composting container with some gutter sealant and black bituminous paint. The super-insulated container keeps the compost much hotter and works amazingly well if the ingredients are emptied and re-mixed with plenty of air worked in. It runs wetter and, unless dryish material is mixed in, an ooze accumulates which can then be tapped off and diluted for use as a liquid feed.

Materials for composting

The composting process will rapidly break down almost all natural materials, including old clothes made of natural fibres and wetted newspaper. Large lumps of wood, bone or fat will decay too slowly and should be broken up or buried. Dry, twiggy material will compost if chopped up and mixed with some nitrogenous material, such as fresh manure. Thorny material is better burned, material containing seeds is best put in the middle of a heap, or burned, and live weeds of a pernicious nature can be killed first by wilting them on a path or sheet of plastic before mixing them in. Alternatively such weeds and seeds can first be drowned for a month or two in a butt of water before adding them to the compost heap. Diseased material may be composted, but only if you are confident that your heap will 'cook' well; otherwise it is safer to burn it.

Leafmould

The leaves of deciduous trees and shrubs can be rotted down on their own to make soil-enriching leafmould.

A simple wire container, made from chicken wire stretched between four upright posts that have been driven into the ground, makes a suitable leafmould bin.

A fast, space-saving alternative is to pack the layers of leaves into black polythene sacks that have been perforated to allow in air. Filled and tied at the top, the sacks should be stood in an out-of-the-way corner until the following spring, by when the contents, gathered the previous autumn, will have turned into good leafmould. Leaves that are kept in outdoor bins may take longer to break down.

Below: Rake up leaves in autumn and rot them down to make leafmould or you can add them to the compost heap.

Compost materials

Note that glass, plastic and metal will not break down and should not be added to your compost heap.

Materials	Speed of composting	Notes
Bedding plants	Slow	
Bracken	Intermediate	Do not use when spores are visible
Cardboard	Slow	
Comfrey leaves	Fast	A good activator
Flowers	Intermediate	
Fruit and vegetable scraps	Intermediate	
Grass mowings	Fast	Mix in well to avoid 'capping'
Hedge clippings (soft)	Intermediate	Valuable for minerals
Hedge clippings (woody)	Slow	Chip or shred before adding
Herbaceous plants	Intermediate	
Leaves (deciduous)	Slow	
Nettles	Fast	A good activator
Newspaper	Slow	Soaks up liquids
Poultry manure	Fast	High in nitrogen
Rhubarb leaves	Intermediate	
Seaweed	Fast	Adds trace elements and encourages bacterial breakdown
Straw (old)	Slow	Soak thoroughly if dry
Straw-based animal manure	Intermediate	Valuable fertility in this
Tea and coffee grounds	Intermediate	
Tea bags	Intermediate	
Vegetable stems (tough)	Intermediate	Cut into small pieces
Weeds, annual	Fast	Only add seeds if heap will get hot enough to kill them
Weeds, perennial	Intermediate	Kill weeds before adding to heap

Weeds and seeds can be drowned for a month or two in a butt of water before adding to the compost heap

gallons of water to flush such a rich source of fertility into the sea.

Saved in a bucket, it makes a superb compost activator; alternatively, each day's quota can be diluted down about 20:1 and watered on last thing at night to feed lawns and increase the cuttings for use elsewhere.

Below: Leaves layered into black polythene sacks and then left for several months will turn into an enriching leafmould.

Above: Nettles have many positive qualities: they attract beneficial insects to the garden and they compost quickly too.

Although some people are squeamish, it is sensible to recycle urine if local regulations do not forbid it. This is not a health hazard in temperate climates, and it is wasteful to use a couple of

Easy composting

Perhaps the biggest drawback to effective composting is the problem of accumulating enough material to make an effective heap – the bigger the mass the more heat is retained and the better it composts.

Rather than store material until enough is available, I spread mine on the ground for the hens to rummage through, and their feet pack it down. Later I scrape it up and put it in the bins to break down. If you don't have hens, it is probably best kept in plastic bags until ready to be combined, but most people just put it in layers in a bin and dig it out and mix it when enough has built up.

A heap will always make better compost if it is re-made after a week and the inside exchanged for the outside. Doing this again after another week will be of further benefit. Each turning mixes the ingredients and stirs in air which then speeds up the process. Do not pack a heap down as this has the opposite effect. There are commercial rotary composters which speed up the process, but these are better suited to warmer climates.

Where there is little material available at any time, there are alternatives to the conventional heap. Co-operation with several neighbours can allow each to make a heap in turn or to share in yours. Another method is pit composting. Dig a hole and put the compost material in, covering each layer with a thin layer of soil. Once the hole is full and proud start another and use the first for growing really hungry feeders on, such as marrows, courgettes, runner beans or potatoes, for a year or two. The pit can then be dug out and the rotted material used as compost.

Worm compost

Making worm compost is an ideal way of using up household waste in winter when material rots down slowly on the compost heap because of the cold. The waste has to be chopped up finely and added a little at a time to a large container containing red brandling worms. (You can buy these or unearth them from a manure or compost heap, or from under a plank or carpet laid on the ground.)

Put the worms in a layer of moist peat or leafmould in the bottom of the container and keep in the warm (in the garage, for example). The container should have air holes in the top, and drainage holes and a drip tray to catch any liquids that ooze out. This liquid makes a good feed when diluted. The worms convert the vegetable waste to a rich material that is best mixed in when planting hungry feeders or that can be added to potting composts.

The worms will die if dug out with the material and put in the soil, so carefully sift them and return them to the container. The worms will not deal with a large quantity of matter at a time, so they are better for small households or for use in conjunction with another container or with a conventional compost heap. Avoid large amounts of citrus peel and dairy produce.

Step 3

Avoid chemicals

The conventional solution to pests and diseases relies heavily on sprays, which drench plants and soil with chemical poisons. Organic gardeners try instead to help plants to resist attacks in the first place by manipulating the natural system of checks and balances in their favour. Pesticides, even organic ones, are used only as a last resort.

Controlling pests and diseases

The aim of the organic gardener is control, not elimination. The gardener makes life difficult for pests and diseases so that plants and crops thrive in spite of them. Organic gardeners aim to prevent pests and diseases from reaching the point where an organically approved pesticide might be needed by building up a wide variety of plants, by creating stable ecosystems and by encouraging predators and parasites.

Growing healthy plants

The primary task in organic gardening is to grow healthy plants that resist attacks and endure minor infestations in much the same way that healthy humans shrug off a cold.

Of all the checks to growth, water imbalance is probably the most common. Desiccated plants will die, but if they even reach wilt point their growth will be severely checked. Waterlogging can be equally serious, especially in cold, low-light conditions. Plants in containers are as often sickened by overwatering in winter and spring as they are by drought in summer.

Air and light are also important factors in preventing infection: each plant must be given

The aim of the organic gardener is control, not elimination

Organic pesticides

Organic gardeners prefer not to use poisonous substances unless they are needed to save a valuable crop. However, they are there as a last resort, though you must take great care not to disrupt ecosystems that have slowly built up. Follow the instructions on the packaging as to their uses, application rates and timing, and precautions, and keep them in a safe place.

Pesticides	Advantages	Disadvantages
Bordeaux mixture	• An inorganic chemical allowed under organic standards as it is not harmful to humans or soil life • Effective against potato blight, peach leaf curl, raspberry cane spot and many other fungal diseases	• It is a preventative, not a cure, and must be applied thoroughly and in good time
Derris	•Liquid or dust, which kills most insects, but is particularly effective against mites • Treat wasps' nests by puffing the dust into the entrance at dusk; repeat after a week	• Indiscriminate in action • Lethal to fish, pigs and tortoises • Breaks down in sunlight • Slower to act than pyrethrum • Currently under review and no longer recommended for use in UK and elsewhere
Insecticidal soap	• The preferred pesticide and even more effective than soft soap • Safe to use and made from natural products	• Ineffective against larger insect pests
Pyrethrum	• Useful for killing many insect pests, including small caterpillars	• No longer available in pure form and commonly supplied with a synthetic synergist • Kills beneficial insects and fish (but is safe for mammals)
Quassia	• Solution (made from a tree bark) that kills aphids but is harmless to bees and other beneficial insects • Sold combined with derris, which makes both more effective	• No longer available on its own
Soft soap	• Traditionally used as a spray to kill aphids, red spider mites, mealy bugs, whiteflies and other pests	
Sulphur	• The pure element is allowed under organic standards as a control for powdery mildews on fruit, flowers and vegetables and for preventing rots in overwintering bulbs and tubers	• Take care when using it with fruit trees and bushes as a few varieties are allergic to sulphur • Read the label and instructions

sufficient space. Never crowd plants – grow a few well rather than many poorly. Vigorous and woody plants need pruning or tying in to allow in air and light, and to allow access for useful predators.

Hygiene

Regular inspection of all parts of the garden, followed by prompt action to remove infected material, will significantly reduce further pest and

Below: A cluster of sempervivums flower in front of golden feverfew, flowering parsley and rosemary. Decorative herbs can be mixed with ornamentals.

disease attacks. For example, the removal of any infested tips controls aphid attacks on broad beans and the prompt removal and burning or deep burial of infected branches prevents the spread of coral spot. Secateurs, saws and knives should be sterilized with surgical spirit to prevent cross-infection occurring.

Take care not to introduce any problems with bought-in plants, manures or dirty tools. Keep new plants in isolation for a week or two. Never buy soil-grown brassica plants because of the danger of clubroot.

There is no need to become over-fastidious with hygiene, however: a small level of pest infestation is necessary to maintain predator populations. It is a good idea to keep things in proportion: the prime cause of loss in the garden is bad weather. Bad practices, such as overcrowding and poor weed control, come a close second. Pests come third, with birds worst of all. Most other pests and diseases are far less common or troublesome.

Direct action

In addition to building self-regulating systems, you will occasionally need to take direct action – and the earlier that action is taken the more effective it will be.

What must also be considered is the economics, in time, cash and labour, of any measure you take in relation to the increase in yield. For example, flea beetles make shot holes in radish and brassica seedlings: maintaining moist conditions reduces their damage and is worthwhile, but spraying may cost more than a radish crop is worth.

Basics of biological control

Bought-in predators have been used commercially for some time, and many are now available to gardeners. Many pests can be controlled by sprinkling on a water-borne parasite, usually a microscopic worm called a nematode; the soil needs to be moist and warm for this to work. For example, leatherjackets can be parasitized by *Steinernema feltiae* nematodes applied to soil in summer. Most biological controls are more suitable for greenhouses, where pests are difficult to control because of the absence of natural predators. Once they are introduced, of course, the use of pesticides has to stop. They are most effective if introduced early in the season, but not before the pest has appeared or the parasites will starve. Full instructions come in the packets.

Most widely used are the controls for whiteflies, red spider mites, aphids and mealybugs.

Biological controls

Pest	Control
Aphids	**Greenhouse:** Once the temperature is above 10°C (50°F) introduce *Aphidoletes aphidomyza* (predatory midge) or *Aphidius* (parasitic wasp) **Garden:** Tap lacewing larvae onto infected plants Introduce lacewing 'hotel' for overwintering
Caterpillars	**Greenhouse:** Introduce *Bacillus thuringiensis* (bacterium) in the evening
Mealybugs	**Greenhouse:** Introduce *Cryptolaemus montrouzieri* (predatory ladybird) on large plants and *Hypoaspis miles* (predatory mite) on small plants when the temperature is above 11°C (52°F)
Red spider mites	**Greenhouse:** If the temperature is above 16°C (61°F) introduce *Phytoseiulus persimilis* (predatory mite) at first sign of infestation
Scale insects	**Greenhouse:** When the temperature is above 14°C (57°F) introduce *Steinernema* (nematode) or *Metaphycus helvolus* (parasitic wasp)
Sciarid flies	**Greenhouse:** Introduce *Hypoaspis miles* (predatory mite) when the temperature is above 11°C (52°F)
Slugs	**Greenhouse:** When the soil temperature is above 5°C (41°F) apply *Phasmarhabditis hermaphrodita* (pathogenic nematode) every six weeks
Thrips	**Greenhouse:** Introduce *Ambleysius* (predatory mite) from late spring
Vine weevils	**Greenhouse:** When the compost temperature is over 12°C (54°F) apply *Heterorhabditis megidis* or *Steinernema carpocapsae* (pathogenic nematodes) **Garden:** When the soil temperature is over 12°C (54°F) apply pathogenic nematodes
Whiteflies	**Greenhouse:** Once the temperature is above 10°C (50°F) introduce *Encarsia formosa* (parasitic wasp) at first sign of infestation

Practical preventative measures

Many simple mechanical methods can be used to exclude pests and reduce their numbers. These cause little harm to the environment, and many can be made from recycled materials.

Hand-picking is effective against many pests. Gooseberry sawflies or cabbage caterpillars, for example, can be dealt with in this way, and many minor infestations can be squeezed with finger and thumb. Slugs and snails come out on warm, wet evenings, and they tend to return to the same site, so they can be spotted with a torch and picked off. Battery-operated vacuum cleaners are excellent for rounding up flying insects, such as whiteflies or flea beetles, which jump when disturbed. Use the jet from a garden hose to knock aphids and other pests off plants; some may return but many will not. This works well in combination with sticky bands (see page 36).

> Use the jet from a garden hose to knock aphids and other pests off plants

Nets

Nets are the best way of protecting fruit. A complete cage is best and makes economic sense, but any pieces of net can be used to protect a branch or two and can be held in place with clothes pegs. The netting bags that fruit and nuts come in are good for individual fruits and bunches, and the feet of nylon stockings and tights do as well. Whole stockings or tights can be pulled over long branches of fruit such as redcurrants. Fine mesh bags can exclude wasps as well as birds, but may encourage mould or botrytis.

Fine netting, woven fleeces and punctured plastic sheets can be used to keep pests off vegetables and fruit and are effective at preventing carrot fly attacks. This fly, about the size of a housefly, has to lay its eggs next to the seedling, so a barrier gives 100 per cent control. The same materials can also be used to protect cabbages from root flies and butterfly caterpillars, and to keep birds off beetroot and salad crops. Carrot root flies can be stopped by a simple barrier or netting. Anything 60–90cm (2–3ft) high around small beds stops the fly, which will go round rather than over.

Carpet squares

Cabbage root flies need to lay their eggs in the soil next to the stem. A barrier made of 13cm (5in) squares of old carpet, tarred roofing felt or cardboard fitting snugly around the stem will seal the soil underneath and prevent access.

Carpet can be used to seal larger areas, trapping insect pests underneath when they emerge from hibernation or their pupae. This can considerably reduce infestations of gooseberry sawflies, raspberry beetles and pear midges. Carpet laid on a wet lawn will bring leatherjackets and other soil pests to the surface overnight. They can be swept up or left to the birds in the morning.

Top: A square of cardboard, carpet or tarred roofing felt is an effective barrier against cabbage root flies.

Above: Cut a slot in each piece of cardboard and fix one around the stem of each plant.

Bands

Bands made of cloth, carpet and corrugated cardboard tied around trunks and stems simulate shredding bark and attract many insects. Examine your catch: beneficial ladybirds can be retained and released to continue their good work in the garden, while the unwelcome pests are evicted.

Earwig traps

Many creatures, especially earwigs, will crawl into hollow bamboo tubes and can then be blown out into a bucket. Earwigs are especially attracted to straw-filled flowerpots on sticks.

Sticky boards and flypapers

These are especially good in the greenhouse, where they trap many pests, especially whiteflies and thrips. Different colours attract different insects: white attracts sawflies; blue attracts thrips; and yellow attracts whiteflies. They are even more effective if they are given a pheromone scent. Hung in the trees, these sticky boards are a good way of reducing codling moth and plum fruit moth attacks.

> Earwigs are attracted to straw-filled flowerpots on sticks

Wasp traps

Wasps are beneficial in the early season as they hunt other insects in great numbers, but in late summer they turn their attention to fruit and should be trapped. A bottle half-full of water and jam should be given a foil cap pierced with a small hole that allows the wasps to crawl in but not to fly out. Do not use traps near flowers or with honey, because bees may also be lured in.

> Carpet laid on a wet lawn will bring leatherjackets and other soil pests to the surface overnight

Slug traps

Slugs can be stopped in their tracks by barriers
of wood ash, pine needles, sharp grit or sawdust.
They are also reluctant to climb over rings
10–13cm (4–5in) high cut from plastic bottles
and set into the ground.

Slugs can be trapped in slug pubs, saucers or
yogurt pots half-full of fermenting beer, in which
they obligingly drown themselves. Sink the pots or
saucers up to their rims in the soil. Friendly
ground beetles, however, also drown unless you
give them some twigs to climb out on. Slugs and
snails also collect under melon or orange
shells and upturned saucers.

Lures

It is possible to make lures for many pests. Tins or
yogurt cartons buried in the ground with bits of
potato or carrot in the base will attract mostly
millipedes and woodlice; slugs and snails will
come to fruit, and wireworms will come to bran
or germinating grain. Dead-fall traps follow the
same principal but without the lure of fruit or
vegetables to entice pests.

Sticky bands

The bands stop pests climbing up tree trunks,
which few predators need to do. They are
especially effective against the female winter
moth (which cannot fly), earwigs and ants. Ants
farm aphids, moving them to tender shoots and
milking them for honeydew. A sticky band reduces
aphid populations because the ants cannot tend
and protect them. Sticky bands can be applied to
the bark of old trees, but on young bark they are
better used on top of a foil strip as the sticky
material may soak in.

*Step 1: To apply sticky bands, first wrap a strip of foil
around the trunk of the tree.*

*Step 2: Next add the sticky band material, painting it
on top of the foil in an even layer.*

Step 3: Wrap a band of corrugated cardboard securely around the trunk.

Step 4: Tie the cardboard in place. Any beneficial insects can be simply shaken free.

Isolation trenches

Digging a trench about 25 x 25cm (10 x 10in) around vegetable beds presents mice, slugs and other small creatures with an effective barrier.

Bird scarers

These psychological barriers work for a short time, so use several and change them daily. Scarecrows, glitterbangs (coffee packaging bags are good), unwanted CDs and flashing humming tape (video or cassette is cheaper than the bought tapes) are worth trying. Black cotton, fur-hat cats, garden hose snakes and paper hawks worry them, but not for very long.

Copper tape

A hoop of copper tape around a pot will deter slugs and snails as they do not like to cross it.

Non-set glue

Non-set glue can help to protect plants from vine weevils both indoors and out.

Child and people proofing

Human pests can be the worst of all and their senseless damage is sometimes worse than their thefts. Fences, barriers and locks are sadly now required, especially for succulent fruit. Signs saying 'Beware of the wasps' nests!' can be more effective than 'Keep out'. Dogs are considered the best guards, but geese are as good and have other benefits.

Know your worst enemies:
directory of most common pests

Aphids (1)

Insects (greenflies or blackflies and sometimes other colours) which live in fast-growing colonies and feed on plants' sap, weakening them and distorting growth. They also transmit viral diseases.

• Spray with soft soap or insecticidal soap.

• Pick off infected leaves and prune out infested shoots.

• Encourage natural predators, especially hoverflies.

Apple sawflies (2)

Cocoons in soil hatch out in spring. Adult flies lay eggs in open blossom. Larvae tunnel into fruitlets, feeding on flesh and seeds. Affected fruitlets drop early; mature fruit has characteristic ribbon scarring.

• Pick up and destroy infected fruitlets as soon as you notice scarring.

Asparagus beetles (3)

Beetles and their larvae feed on foliage and stems from late spring on. Persistent attacks may check growth.

• In autumn clear away plant debris, which is where beetles overwinter.

Big bud mites (4)

Mites breed inside developing buds of blackcurrants, causing them to become round and swollen. Mites carry reversion disease (see page 48), which causes slow deterioration of bush and poor cropping.

• Remove and burn all swollen buds before spring.

• In severe cases cut back all growth to ground level and burn cuttings.

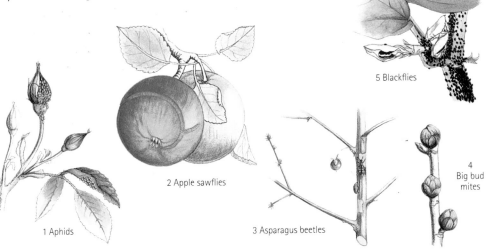

5 Blackflies

4 Big bud mites

2 Apple sawflies

3 Asparagus beetles

1 Aphids

Blackflies (5)

These aphids cluster on growing tips of broad beans in late spring and can spread to rest of plant, stunting growth and reducing crop. May spread to other beans, beetroot, chard and ornamentals.
• Sow hardy varieties in autumn so that plants are tougher and less attractive in spring.
• Pinch out affected tips.
• Spray with soft soap.

Cabbage root flies (6)

Larvae eat roots, causing stunted, wilting plants. They overwinter as shiny brown cocoons in soil and emerge to lay eggs around plants.
• Grow plants under fine netting or fleece or lay 13cm (5in) square mats of carpet underlay around plants so that they fit snugly around stems.
• Intercrop with beans in alternate rows to confuse pest.
• Dig over soil in winter after infected crop.

Cabbage white caterpillars (7)

Large, plump caterpillars feed on leaves and bore into the hearts of cabbages and lettuces.
• Pick off the caterpillars by hand.
• Grow plants under fine netting or fleece to stop butterflies laying eggs on undersides of leaves.
• Spray with *Bacillus thuringiensis* (bacterium), which kills caterpillars but is harmless to humans.

Carrot flies (8)

Larvae feed on roots of carrot and other root vegetables. Seedlings may be killed; older plants will be stunted. Roots are tunnelled through with white larvae inside. Flies overwinter in soil and in roots left in ground.
• Sow in early spring or midsummer.
• Grow carrots under fine netting or fleece or erect a barrier of fine netting about 75cm (30in) high around plot .
• Lift and destroy infested plants immediately.

Codling moths (9)

Affect mainly apples, pears and quinces. Adults hatch from cocoons in midsummer to lay eggs in leaves or fruit. Caterpillars tunnel into maturing fruit and feed for several weeks before pupating.
• Hang pheromone traps, containing a sticky substance that attracts male moths, in trees.

7 Cabbage white caterpillars

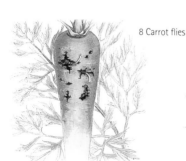

8 Carrot flies

6 Cabbage root flies

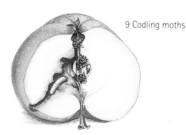

9 Codling moths

Cutworms (10)

Moth caterpillars live in the soil and feed at night on the soil's surface, eating young plants at soil level and attacking stems and roots of vegetables and strawberries.

- Protect individual plants with collars.
- Hoe and dig regularly in winter to expose them to birds.
- Pick them off by hand at night.

Earwigs (11)

Earwigs attack fruit trees (especially apples) and flowers. They do eat codling moth eggs and woolly aphids, so should be left if possible.

- If a problem trap them in flowerpots filled with straw and supported upside down on canes.

Flea beetles (12)

Attacks cabbages and other brassicas, covering leaves with small holes. The beetles hibernate in plant debris and under loose tree bark.

- Cover plants with fine netting or woven fleece.
- Go along rows with sticky greased board because beetles jump up when disturbed.
- Spray with pyrethrum.

Leatherjackets (13)

The larvae of craneflies live in the soil and are mainly a problem on vegetable plots dug from old lawns or old pasture land or on very weedy plots. They feed on vegetable roots (especially those of brassicas).

- Keep soil weed-free.
- Hoe and dig the soil regularly to expose them to the birds.

Mealybugs (14)

Cacti, succulents and many other plants, especially under glass, are often affected. Pinkish grey, soft-bodied insects suck sap from young stems. In heavy infestation foliage and fruit are sticky with honeydew, on which black sooty mould develops.

- Spray with pyrethrum.
- Under glass introduce *Cryptolaemus montrouzieri* (predatory ladybird).

11 Earwigs

13 Leatherjackets

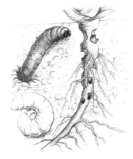

10 Cutworms

12
Flea beetles

14 Mealybugs

Onion flies (15)

Resembling small houseflies, these attack onions, leeks and shallots. Eggs are laid near the base of seedlings, and maggots bore into young bulbs, causing leaves to turn yellow. Remove infected plants to limit spread.

• Dig over infected land in winter to destroy the larvae.
• Grow seedlings under fine netting or fleece.

Pea moths (16)

Caterpillars live and feed inside pea pods. Moth lays eggs in midsummer on flowering pea plants. Caterpillars eat their way into developing pods.

• Sow peas early and late to avoid midsummer flowering time.
• Dig over infested soil in winter to disturb pupating caterpillars.
• Protect plants in flower with fine netting or woven fleece.

Pear midges (17)

Females lay eggs in unopened flower buds. Larvae hatch out within developing fruitlets. After petal fall fruitlets turn black and drop. Maggots then crawl into soil to pupate.

• Collect and compost all fallen fruitlets.
• Remove affected fruitlets as soon as noticed.
• Dig over soil near affected trees in winter to expose cocoons to birds.

Pea weevils (18)

Also affects beans, chewing a scalloped edge on leaves. Not a serious problem on strong plants, but young plants may die back. The weevils overwinter in plant debris and larvae emerge as adults in midsummer.

• Encourage strong, fast growth.
• Sow beans under cover and plant out when growing strongly.

Raspberry beetles (19)

Adults feed on raspberry blossom in late spring. Larvae tunnel into ripening fruit and may not be noticed until fruit is picked. Pupae overwinter in soil near canes.

• Lightly hoe soil in autumn and winter to expose pupae to birds.

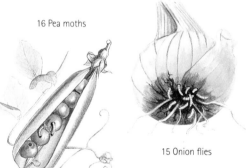

16 Pea moths

15 Onion flies

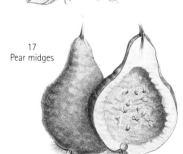

17 Pear midges

19 Raspberry beetles

18 Pea weevils

Red spider mites (20)

Usually a greenhouse pest but can attack strawberries, raspberries and currants in hot weather. The undersurfaces of leaves become bronzed; older leaves are withered or crisp. Greenish mites are visible with magnification.
• Cut off all leaves after harvesting fruit.
• Use *Phytoseiulus persimilis* (predatory mite) in greenhouses.

Scale insects (21)

Small, flat insects attach themselves to fruit and other trees, vines and ornamental plants under glass. They suck sap and smear leaves with honeydew, which encourages sooty mould.
• Spray with insecticidal soap.
• Use *Metaphycus helvolus* (predatory wasp).

Stem eelworms (22)

Attack a wide range of fruit, vegetables and ornamental plants. Onion and leek leaves swell and distort, and bulbs crack and rot. Eelworm survives in the soil for a considerable time. There is no cure for infected plants.
• Burn all infected plants.
• Grow only brassicas and lettuces on infested plot for two years.
• Keep area weed-free.

Vine weevils (23)

Beetles feed on leaf margins of many plants, especially rhododendrons, euonymus and hydrangeas. Plump white maggots attack roots, especially of container-grown plants, and tubers of ornamental plants under glass. The roots are usually destroyed and plants will not recover.
• Use *Heterorhabditis megidis* or *Steinernema carpocapsae* (pathogenic nematodes) applied in late summer.

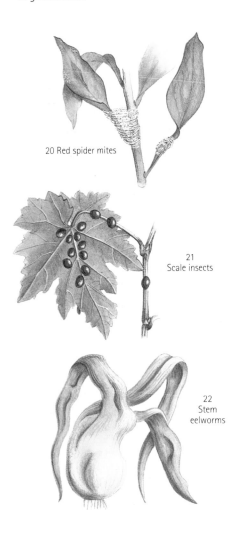

20 Red spider mites

21 Scale insects

22 Stem eelworms

23 Vine weevils

Wasps (24)

A pest only in high summer and early autumn, when fruit is damaged, and especially in hot, dry weather, when numbers increase.
- Suspend wasp traps in trees.

Whiteflies (25)

Small, winged insects, which live on leaves of brassicas and fly up in clouds when disturbed. Young scales remain on the plants.
- Dig up winter brassicas as soon as cropping is finished and bury in trench or compost heap before planting out new ones.
- Remove leaves with visible scales before they turn into adults.
- Suck up adults with mini-vacuum cleaner.
- Spray with insecticidal soap.
- Under glass use *Encarsia formosa* (parasitic wasp) at first sign of infestation.

Wireworms (26)

Larvae of the click beetle, which lays eggs in grass or weedy soil. Attack stems and tubers of many vegetables (including onions, potatoes, carrots, peas and beans). More of a problem on old pasture land.
- Keep land cultivated to expose them to birds.
- Catch them on small pieces of carrot or potato spiked on sticks and buried and renewed regularly.

Woolly aphids (27)

A species that attacks tree trunks, branches and twigs. Aphid covers itself with white, wool-like covering. Attacked wood becomes swollen and may crack, allowing entry to canker and other diseases; soft, lumpy galls appear on bark.
- Spray with soft soap or insecticidal soap.
- If this does not work, cut out infestation.

25 Whiteflies

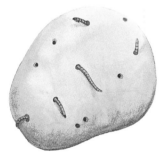

26 Wireworms

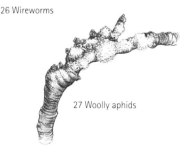

27 Woolly aphids

24 Wasps

Know your worst enemies:
directory of most common diseases

American gooseberry mildew (1)

Also affects blackcurrants. Powdery, white coating on leaves, shoots and fruits; patches become brown and felted.

- Avoid overcrowded bushes and weedy soil.
- Prune regularly to keep bushes open and to admit light and air.
- Cut out and burn diseased shoots.
- Spray with Bordeaux mixture at flower stage.

Apple canker (2)

Destructive disease (also of plums and pears), causing sunken, discoloured patches on bark; branches become swollen. White pustules appear in summer and small, red fruiting bodies appear in winter.

- Cut out and burn diseased patches, branches or shoots, cutting back to clean wood.
- Feed and mulch to encourage vigour.

Bacterial canker (3)

A serious disease of plums, with bacteria living in the leaves. Elongated cankers on branches exude gum; leaves have brown, circular spots; buds fail to open on cankered branches; if leaves develop, they yellow and drop as branch dies back.

- Cut out and burn affected wood.
- Spray with Bordeaux mixture in midsummer and again in early and mid-autumn.

3 Bacterial canker

1 American gooseberry mildew

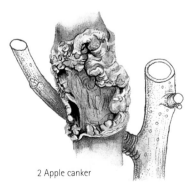

2 Apple canker

44   AVOID CHEMICALS

Blackleg (4)

A bacterial disease of potatoes, causing foliage to turn yellow and stems to blacken and die. Tubers may also be affected, developing a brown, slimy rot inside.

- Remove and burn affected plants.
- Lift the rest of the crop to avoid contact with infected tubers.
- Do not save any tubers for seed.
- Buy only certified seed to avoid blackleg.

Botrytis (5)

A common greenhouse problem of grapes, strawberries, cucumbers, tomatoes and lettuces. Affected plants are covered with a velvety, grey-brown fungus, which thrives in cold, damp conditions.

- Remove dead leaves and over-ripe fruit.
- Ventilate to reduce humidity.
- Water in the morning, not at night.
- Do not overwater.
- Use fertilizers sparingly.

Clubroot (6)

Disease (mainly of brassicas) causing wilting, stunted plants. When pulled up, roots are swollen and distorted. Clubroot prefers acid conditions and can stay in the ground for 20 years.

- Dig up and burn affected plants.
- Practise good crop rotation and never grow brassicas in infected soil.
- Keep ground well limed.
- Raise seedlings in pots to get them off to a good start.
- Never buy in seedlings.

> Clubroot prefers acid conditions and can stay in the ground for 20 years

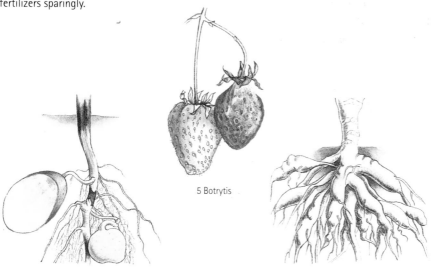

5 Botrytis

4 Blackleg

6 Clubroot

Cucumber mosaic virus (7)

Affects cucurbits (especially marrows) and is spread by aphids. Diseased plants are stunted and have puckered, distorted leaves with yellow mottling on them.

- Destroy infected plants immediately.
- Encourage aphid predators by planting marigolds and nasturtiums in the vegetable garden.

Damping off (8)

A fungal disease that causes seedlings to collapse at ground level. Troublesome where seedlings are overcrowded or growing in wet, compacted soil.

- Sow seeds thinly and use sterilized soil or compost with a good tilth.
- Avoid overwatering.
- Use clean tapwater (not from a tank or butt, which may contain infective organisms).

Fireblight (9)

Bacterial disease affecting various trees and shrubs. Cankers appear at base of dead shoots and red-brown discoloration appears inside. Causes dieback or browning of leaves.

- Cut out diseased wood 60cm (2ft) below affected tissue.
- Disinfect pruning tools after use.

Leaf spot (10)

Many plants affected, especially in wet seasons. Leaf surface can become completely brown and shrivelled; plant loses vigour.

- Remove and burn diseased leaves.
- Spray plants with Bordeaux mixture.
- If brassicas are affected, remove alternate plants to improve ventilation.
- Do not over-use nitrogen-rich fertilizer.

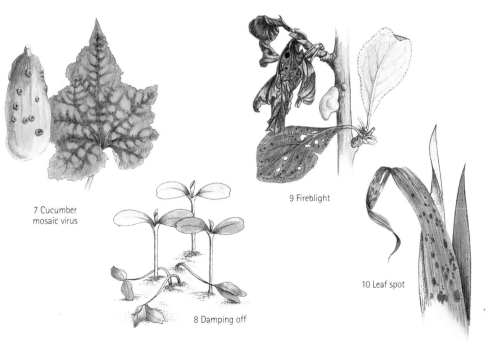

7 Cucumber mosaic virus

8 Damping off

9 Fireblight

10 Leaf spot

Mildew (11)

Downy and powdery mildews are seen as pale grey fungus on leaves, flowers and young shoots. Affects many ornamentals, including roses. Downy mildew affects vines and vegetables.

- Remove and burn affected leaves.
- Spray with Bordeaux mixture.
- Avoid overcrowding and humid conditions.

Peach leaf curl (12)

Leaves become thickened and curl; red blisters develop and are covered with fungal spores. Leaves fall early, and tree is weakened. Fungus overwinters in bark or on shoots. The spores are carried by rain.

- Spray with Bordeaux mixture in late winter or early spring (repeating 10–14 days later) to prevent spores from entering buds.
- Spray again just before leaf fall.
- Erect polythene cover over espalier and fan-trained trees to keep off rain.

Potato blight (13)

Causes brown patches on leaves, especially in warm, wet weather; foliage blackens and dies; tubers may rot. Spreads rapidly in humid conditions.

- Spray with Bordeaux mixture at fortnightly intervals until harvesting.
- In severe cases, cut down and burn foliage.
- Delay harvesting for two or three weeks so tubers are not affected.
- Grow resistant cultivars such as 'Cara', 'Wilja' and 'Kondor'.

12 Peach leaf curl

11 Mildew

13 Potato blight

Reversion disease (14)

Carried by big bud mites (see page 38), which attack blackcurrants. Difficult to recognize, but leaves are narrower than usual and have fewer than five pairs of veins on the main lobe. Flower buds turn bright magenta (instead of grey), bushes lose vigour and crop is reduced. There is no known cure.

• Dig up and burn affected plants.
• Plant certified disease-free stock on a different site.

Rose black spot (15)

Common fungal disease, especially in wet, humid weather. Leaf spots may merge into large, dead areas; leaves wither and die.

• Prune hard in autumn and burn prunings to kill off overwintering spores.
• Pick up and burn fallen leaves in autumn.
• Mulch soil well.
• Plant roses in a sunny, open site and space well to ensure good ventilation.

Rust (16)

Affects a wide range of plants. Leaves and stems develop red, brown or yellow pustules. Leaves may wither and die. Whole plant may wilt.

• Remove and burn affected leaves and whole plant if severely affected.
• Spray plants with sulphur.
• Under glass improve ventilation to reduce humidity and make sure water droplets do not remain on leaves.

> Plant roses in a sunny, open site and space well to ensure good ventilation

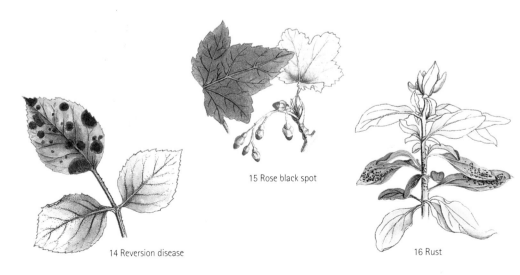

15 Rose black spot

14 Reversion disease

16 Rust

Scab (17)

Disease affecting potatoes and causing ugly, ragged scabs on the skin. Most often found in dry, sandy soil lacking organic matter.

• Dig in plenty of humus (compost or manure) and do not lime soil before planting.

• Water in dry weather.

• Add a layer of grass clippings to the trench at planting.

• Grow resistant cultivars such as 'Arran Pilot', 'Arran Comet', 'King Edward' or 'Maris Peer'.

Silverleaf (18)

A fungal disease of fruit trees, caused when spores enter through wounds. Leaves become silvered and then brown; progressive dieback affects branches; small, purple, white or brown fruiting bodies develop on dead wood.

• Cut back all dead branches at least 15cm (6in) beyond infection in summer (when there is least chance of new infection).

• Sterilize pruning tools before and after use.

Soft rot (19)

Affects swedes and turnips, particularly in wet weather. Flesh rots into a foul-smelling mess while rind remains intact. Most troublesome on heavily manured and badly drained soil.

• Practise crop rotation.

• Make sure drainage is good and grow on deep beds to improve drainage.

• Control slugs to save foliage because disease can enter through wounds.

• Remove and burn affected plants.

> Sterilize pruning tools before and after use to avoid silverleaf

17 Scab

18 Silverleaf

19 Soft rot

Weeds in the organic garden

Any piece of ground left untended rapidly becomes covered with weeds. As the weeds slowly build up the fertility of the soil, the patch of ground becomes suitable for nettles, brambles and tree seedlings. A profusion of these weeds, especially nettles, can indicate a potentially rich site. Deep-rooted weeds like dock and thistle are also good for the soil as they bring up nutrients, making them available for future crops.

The types of weed will always be those most suited to the conditions, so:

• If they consist of acid-loving plants such as daisies, small nettles and sorrels, the topsoil is probably acid.
• Lime soils are indicated by cowslips, knapweed and silverweed.
• Damp conditions encourage nettles, buttercups, bugle and rushes.
• Lots of docks means that horses or their manure have been on the land as the seeds pass through their intestines unchecked.
• Lots of tomato seedlings could mean that sewage sludge has been used.
• Beware of any land that grows few weeds!

Good weeds and bad weeds

Weeds are, as we are always being told, just plants in the wrong place. Many are otherwise valuable garden plants or even crops – poppies, feverfew and red valerian, for example. Many weeds are edible: chickweed and dandelion leaves are delicious in salads, fat hen, nettles and ground elder can be cooked like spinach, while the roots of dandelion, horseradish and vetch are all edible. In some gardens, weeds may be the last remnants of the original flora and so help preserve insect and wildlife populations. A stand of weeds not only fixes and stabilizes the soil, but can act as a miniature hedge and windbreak, sheltering emerging seedlings, although it should be eradicated before it competes too much.

Remember, too, before you get rid of all weeds that some are attractive to bees, butterflies and insects. They should not be allowed to compete with other plants, of course, but if you have a patch of ground at the end of the garden where they will do no harm, it is worth allowing some to survive. Weeds that attract beneficial insects include nettles, poppies, groundsel, herb robert and dandelion.

Most of all, weeds are a useful source of fertility, admirably suited to their conditions by self-selection. They produce a wealth of green manure at times when other plants cannot use the soil and act as valuable groundcover over winter. They are also superb mineral accumulators, making these accessible to crops after they have been dug in or mulched. Clovers and vetches fix nitrogen, comfrey is well known for accumulating potassium, as are nettles and thistles, while phosphorus is collected by fat hen, sorrel, yarrow and thornapple. Stubborn-rooted perennials, such as comfrey and nettles, will have to be mulched rather than dug in if they are used as green manure – and you will need to dig up the roots later, unless you want an annual crop.

Weed control in non-soil areas

Paths, drives and patios are often a problem because windblown seeds lodge in every niche. Prevention is better than cure, so either point up holes and cracks with cement or mastic (after cleaning them all out by hand with a knife and a pressure hose) or grow plants you want there. Working in a mixture of potting compost and thyme and camomile seeds will prevent other plants getting in. Flame-guns (see page 53) are best where they can safely be used, knives remove weeds from cracks; I use a strimmer to flay them, although the occasional stone has done for a window or two. A carpet or plastic sheet laid on top for a few weeks will kill off many weeds. It can also be laid permanently and covered with fresh gravel.

> Weeds are just plants in the wrong place

Groundcover plants

Mulching (see pages 54–7) under shrubs and over large areas becomes expensive in materials and time as there will always be some weeds that arrive on the wind. It then becomes more effective to use groundcover plants, especially grass which is so simply maintained. Other alternatives include:

• **Ivy** in shady areas; it is easily weeded by strimming anything that grows up out of it.
• Planting out bulbs, primroses, violets and other naturalizing plants can further improve appearances and the wildlife habitat without upsetting weed control: a strimmer can be used up to and around the chosen plants.

• **Mints** are the most vigorous and beneficial groundcover plants wherever height allows; these suppress most weeds and are loved by insects when they flower. They can be kept within bounds by a mown grass path.

Above: Primroses can be naturalized, with or without a carpet of ivy around them, to form groundcover.

Below: Mints make very effective groundcover and their flowers will attract beneficial insects.

Controlling weeds

After grass cutting, weeding probably takes up most gardening time. Weeds will rapidly choke plants and spoil the garden, lock up fertility in seeds and roots, and harbour pests and diseases.

Organic gardeners do not use chemical herbicides, which kill not only weeds but other forms of life as well. As with pests, the aim is control, not elimination, as some weeds have their uses as well as drawbacks.

There are many ways to kill weeds. Some, like digging up, are better used to break new ground, while others, like hoeing, can be used to maintain control. Mulching is probably most important, as it not only prevents weed seeds germinating but conserves the fertility and moisture of the soil.

Hygiene

Take precautions to prevent weeds being brought into your garden – dirty manures, uncomposted mulches and bought-in plants smuggle in seeds.
• Protect flowerbeds, gravel paths and drives by never letting anything set seed nearby or upwind.
• Rotation is as useful. By moving the crop and changing the conditions no weed species is favoured and allowed to become established.

Digging

If you are starting a new border where the ground has been under grass for a while, digging is the best method. Regular grass-cutting will have reduced weed populations, leaving grasses and rosette weeds such as daisies. From early autumn to late winter the turf can be skimmed off and stacked for loam, used elsewhere or dug in. Tap-rooted weeds can be dug up as they are uncovered and wilted for compost. Removing creeping weeds, such as couchgrass, is exceedingly laborious; completely excluding light with a black plastic mulch is easier.
• Dig in overwintering groundcover weeds in the early spring, so that they have time to decay before anything is planted.
• Dig and chop small spits methodically rather than labour with larger pieces.

Rotary cultivating

Rotary cultivating kills earthworms, damages some soil textures and is noisy, dangerous work. It is not really suitable for ground that is badly infested with perennial weeds as most rotavators have insufficient power, and if they succeed they chop roots into many pieces which then regrow. However, they are useful for incorporating green manures and overwintered annual weeds. They are most definitely not for the smaller garden because of their awkwardness in confined spaces. To break in a large plot, which is not compacted and is down to clean turf or light cover, rotavate two or three times in spring, about two weeks apart, to incorporate the cover as well as any regrowth as it occurs.

- Alternatively, lift and invert the surface layer of soil in shallow slices, and hoe after a week or two to prevent the weeds from re-rooting.

Handweeding

Handweeding is the best way to remove weeds from among plants. Kneeling pads protect the knees, and a sharp knife helps cut stubborn roots rather than pulling them up with a large clod. Remove the weeds close to the plants first, then the larger ones between. Small seedling weeds may then be killed with the edge of the knife or a hand rake rather than by pulling them up.

Although it is laborious, you can convert perennial weeds into fertility if the new leaves are pulled off each week until the root system expires. Some much-feared weeds, such as ground elder, can be eliminated in a season if all leaves and shoots are removed weekly.

Hoeing

Severing the top growth just below ground level is most effective, but the hoe must be sharp. In heavy, sticky or stony ground it may pay to put a hoeing mulch of sharp sand or sieved compost on top of the soil to make the going easier.

Hoeing is good for keeping borders clear. Annual weeds need hoeing fortnightly from early spring to late summer, but little thereafter. Hoeing every fortnight takes little time, but if left longer the weeds become established and take more effort. Hoeing is effective against perennial weeds if done weekly, so the top growth is continually hoed off. The roots become exhausted using up their reserves to make new growth, and will die.

Flame-gunning

This is not as frightening as it sounds. A gas or paraffin blowtorch is passed over the weeds to cook but not char the leaves, leaving them to weaken the root system as they wither. It is effective against seedlings, but if the weeds are established some may recover and need a second treatment. It is possible to kill perennial weeds with repeated weekly flame-gunning, though it is more ecological to dig them up and compost them.

Timing a flame-gunning just before a crop emerges can be useful; it removes the weeds without disturbing the crop or bringing up more weed seeds. For example, carrots take 12–18 days to germinate so all weeds emerging in the first 10 days can be removed with a treatment on day 11. The carrots then emerge, deterring further weeds.

Can I use a flame-gun?

✓ For large areas: Yes, it's most useful for this
✓ Seedbeds: Yes
✓ Gravel drives: Yes, but keep away from cars, buildings and inflammable materials
✓ Trees: Yes, just up to large trees' trunks
✓ Brussels sprouts: Yes, if mature
✓ Herbaceous plants: Yes, while dormant if the crown is covered with sand
✓ Rockeries: Yes, use a small blowtorch
✓ Paths and patios: Yes, use a small blowtorch, hot-air paint stripper, boiling water or even a steam iron
✗ Conifers: No
✗ Evergreens: No
✗ Hedges: No
✗ Plants with dead leaves: No

Mulching

Mulching is probably the most important yet under-used method of weed control. Mulching materials can be expensive to buy, but can save much time and effort by suppressing weeds. They will all help moisture conservation, and they encourage growth by helping to maintain a stable soil temperature. Organic mulches, when they are applied regularly, add fertility and also improve the texture of the soil.

All mulches can be applied at any time but are most beneficial if they are applied in spring, when the soil is warming up but before winter rain has evaporated. Mulches which are applied too early will keep the soil cold and slow down growth. If there is a long period of dry weather it is a good idea to rake or roll aside mulches when it rains and replace them afterwards, to prevent the mulch soaking up all the water and stopping it reaching the soil.

Advantages

Mulches are the easiest way of breaking in new ground, as well as a good way of keeping weeds down later. Providing the top growth is not woody and has at least been cut with a rotary mower, an area can be turned into weed-free, clean soil in six months with little effort or preparation.

• All weeds are killed by completely excluding light with impenetrable mulches.

• Tougher perennial weeds are stopped only by thick, opaque plastic or fabric, such as old carpet, but most weeds can be killed off with a thick mulch of straw, hay or grass clippings on top of cardboard and newspaper.

• Avoid using opaque black plastic on areas larger than 1m (3ft) because lack of air and moisture can cause problems with the soil; on these large areas it is better to use perforated black plastic or old carpet.

• It helps if an isolation trench 30cm (12in) deep and wide is dug round the perimeter first and the mulch continued over the edge.

Mulching new ground works best if an impenetrable mulch is put down just as the weeds have started into growth, flattening them underneath – usually in early spring when the soil is also full of water; doing this after mid-spring is far less effective. The weeds turn yellow through lack of light and rapidly rot, followed by their root systems, feeding soil life and increasing fertility. After a month or so the sheet of mulch can be rolled back early in the morning to expose any creatures for the birds. Worms and beneficial insects move quickly and escape, but pests, such as slugs, are slower and do not.

If an area is mulched like this in early spring, it can be cropped from late spring. The weeds may recover if the mulch is simply removed, but some vegetables can be planted out through holes in the mulch, where they will grow wonderfully in the moist, enriched soil underneath. Tomatoes, courgettes, marrows, ridge cucumbers, melons under cloches and sweetcorn will all do well.

> Mulches are the easiest way of breaking in new ground

Top: A carpet mulch gets to work breaking up new ground. This is the result after 10 days.

Middle: This is the result after three weeks. Most of the weeds have now disappeared.

Bottom: After several months the weeds have rotted down and been incorporated into the soil.

if necessary. Almost all the weeds and roots will have rotted and disappeared, leaving a rich texture and natural stratification that may be better left undisturbed. Winter crops can be planted through the mulch, or the plot can be overwintered under a green manure, which has the advantage of restoring the pH of the soil (which tends to drop under mulches).

In the same way, green manures and overwintered weeds can be mulched in early spring with sheets of plastic or fabric or even under large quantities of grass clippings. Again, crops can then be planted through the mulch into the enriched soil in late spring. Compost can be added as well before mulching for optimum results when growing hungry feeders.

Impenetrable or loose mulches can be applied onto bare soil or annual weeds in the vegetable plot in the autumn months.

• They protect the soil from erosion and encourage soil life, especially earthworms, so that when the mulch is removed or planted through in spring the soil will have excellent texture and very good fertility.

• Autumn mulching can benefit herbaceous and less hardy plants by protecting them from frost, although plants subject to rot in damp conditions should be mulched only with light, airy materials, such as loose straw or bracken.

Brassicas also thrive, but most of these plants occupy the land through winter so do not fit in if the area is needed for autumn.

In autumn after any crop has been removed, the mulch can be removed and the area dug over

*Above: Composted or chipped bark makes an
attractive mulch for a path.*

Disadvantages

Mulches do have a few drawbacks other than the
cost, however.

• Sheet mulches may encourage pests underneath,
such as voles, moles and slugs, and loose ones
tend to be scattered onto lawns by birds.

• There is also a danger of rotting crowns or bark
in excessively damp conditions, and grafts may
take root if the union is covered by a mulch.

• Mulches can also seal in the soil warmth and
growth above becomes more prone to frost than
it would over bare soil.

Plastic mulches

Plastic sheets are a great aid to weed control, but
they are unsightly, costly and environmentally
undesirable. Nevertheless, they have a number of
uses in the organic garden. Clear plastic, similar
to that used for polytunnels, can be pinned to the
ground to warm up the soil in spring and
encourage flushes of weeds. Black or opaque
plastic sheet, thick enough to exclude all light,
warms the soil and kills weeds, even perennials. It
can be laid permanently and then covered with a
loose mulch of wood chippings to improve the
appearance so that it is suitable for shrub borders,
soft fruit and other permanent plantings. In the
same way it can be laid under gravel paths and
drives. Use perforated plastic on large areas to
prevent water problems and lack of aeration to
the soil. Black-and-white plastic sheets are useful:
after the black surface has warmed the soil and
killed weeds it can be reversed to the white side
to reflect light onto the plants and confuse pests.

• Squares of plastic, with a slit for access and the
edges buried in soil, make a superb mulch for
young trees, keeping them weed-free and
preventing evaporation for a year or two.

• Long strips 1m (3ft) or so wide are excellent for
starting hedges; cuttings of easy rooters such as
quickthorn can even be pushed through them.

• Strips of plastic can also be used for
strawberries, vegetables and particularly lettuces,
which then get less dirty, though slugs may
become more of a problem.

All plastic sheets have to be well anchored
with earth or stones, otherwise in high winds
there is a danger of them and the plants blowing
away or becoming damaged.

Types of mulch

Material	Type	Advantages	Disadvantages
Cocoa shells	Loose	• High in nitrogen • Very good at deterring slugs	• Should be laid to a depth of about 5cm (2in) to be effective • Light and easily blown initially
Composted bark	Loose	• Attractive	• Scattered by birds • Expensive for large areas • Should be laid to a depth of about 8cm (3in) to be effective
Sand and Gravel	Loose	• Attractive • Suitable for plants that like Mediterranean-type conditions	• Will not improve soil fertility
Leafmould	Loose	• Homemade • Use over a sheet mulch	• Better used in potting composts
Paper and cardboard	Sheet	• Readily available and free • Useful for keeping salad crops clean in the greenhouse • Good for keeping down weed growth when used under another material • Used under loose material will prevent birds mixing weed seeds into the mulch	• Too light in open garden unless used with another mulch or weights on top • Rot rapidly
Plastic sheets	Sheet	• Cheap • Efficient	• Unattractive • Expensive • Environmentally undesirable • Prevents soil aeration
Semi-permeable membrane	Sheet	• Resistant to weed growth • Porosity allows better soil aeration and less water run-off than plastic • Ideal for valuable crops (e.g. strawberries)	• Expensive over large areas • Environmentally dubious
Prunings (woody)	Loose	• Free	• Must be composted before use
Straw and hay	Loose	• Good soil improver	• May include its own seeds
Wood chips	Loose	• Good semi-formal path	• Must be composted for other uses

What weed is that?

There are two types of weed, perennials and annuals, and once the former have been totally eliminated the latter are easy to control with a little time and effort.

Annual weeds

Annual weed seeds germinate as soon as soil is exposed to the light, warmth and wet, but they can be prevented from doing so by mulching or deep burial. As seedlings, these weeds are relatively easy to kill, but they rapidly become tougher. Some can even set seed lying on the ground if they have reached the flowering stage. From the point of view of weed control it doesn't matter if the seedling weed is actually a biennial or annual; it is small and easily killed if it is not long established. These are the best weeds to use as green manure or winter groundcover, as they are not deep-rooting and are easy to eradicate.

Once all the perennial weeds have been cleared from an area there are almost certainly going to be thick flushes of weed seedlings for a year or two, but after some seasons of regular weeding there will be fewer seedlings.

If you want to use annual weeds to give good winter cover on the soil, digging or deep raking will bring up more seeds. Also, selected weeds or other favoured plants can be allowed to seed on vegetable beds and other areas needing cover and the added benefit of green manuring.

Where the weeds are being mulched, dug or hoed in, their goodness is retained. They can also be put on the compost heap, and their fertility thus used for more important crops. All weeds can be composted, but those with pernicious roots should be withered on a path first. Alternatively rot them along with seeding weeds in a butt of water for a few weeks and you get a free liquid feed into the bargain. Diseased weeds are probably best burned.

Perennial weeds

Established perennial weeds survive from year to year by means of underground roots and bulbs, and the worst creep, spread and regrow from pieces of root. Most of them also produce seeds. Weeds such as docks, horseradish and dandelions have long taproots which store food for the plants, bringing up water and nutrients from deep in the soil. Destroying the leaves once is no good, for the root will simply produce new ones. If you cut off the root, leaving even a small piece in the soil, it will grow again, though dock can be killed by taking out the top 10cm (4in) of root.

> Never plant up beds or borders without first removing or killing all perennial weeds

> Where the weeds are being mulched, dug, or hoed in, their goodness is retained

Annual weeds

Shepherd's purse

Groundsel

Hairy bittercress

Annual meadow grass

Creepers such as couchgrass, nettles and ground elder develop a mass of stems just below ground. These have to be dug up, with every small piece of stem removed, for again even a small section of stem left behind will develop new plants.

If you have taken over a new garden or allotment, or are simply breaking in a new piece of ground, it is essential to clear each and every bit of these weeds. Clearing them methodically reduces later weed control effort to the seedling annuals, which can be easily hoed or mulched. Never plant up beds or borders without first removing or killing all perennial weeds – if they are allowed to interpenetrate plant roots, weeding becomes far more difficult.

Perennial weeds

Lesser celandine

Japanese knotweed

Horseradish

Broad-leaved dock

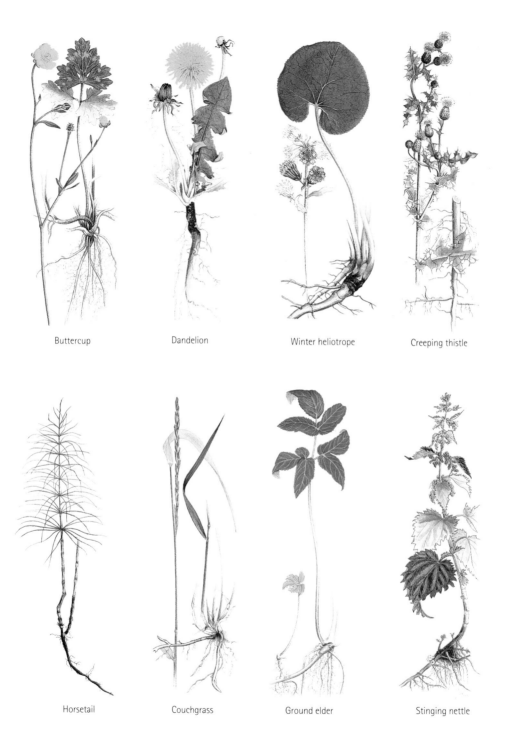

Buttercup

Dandelion

Winter heliotrope

Creeping thistle

Horsetail

Couchgrass

Ground elder

Stinging nettle

Step 4

Choose the right plants

Using good methods is 95 per cent of organic gardening. Plants want to grow, and will if we give them the right conditions. So choose plants that are suited to their local conditions, and avoid those that present obvious problems. There is no point in trying to grow watermelons in a temperate climate, rhododendrons on chalk or cauliflowers in hot, dry, sandy soil. Grow plants that are suited to your soil and climate and they will succeed.

Factors to bear in mind

There are various factors to bear in mind when choosing plants. As well as the general conditions of basic soil type and climate, which will dictate the types of plants, you also need to look at aspect (how much sun the area gets, from which direction, and the amount of exposure to wind) and micro-climate.

Soil type

Both the acidity and moisture-retaining properties of your soil have a profound effect on your general gardening and the former is only easily overcome by growing in containers. You can do a little to alter the acidity of your soil but for many more plants it is better to change their root conditions. This usually means lightening heavy soils to make them warmer and freer-draining to suit the dry sun-lovers, and mucking and mulching light soils to make them suited to heavy feeders and those that tolerate but dislike lime.

Aspect

Much of the skill of gardening lies in selecting plants that will benefit most or endure well the varying conditions a small garden imposes. Most effectively have walls all round and many are tilted away from the sunniest direction. In the northern hemisphere walls facing south are warmest all year round as they get most sun, and this applies to gardens as well. However, one gardener's sunny wall is another's shady one and with small gardens many areas are shady and few sunny. In the border below each wall the conditions are very different and completely different plants will succeed in each. In sunnier south-facing gardens or beds you can obviously succeed better with the many plants that need the most sun, and fruit and vegetables will be sweeter. However, shady north-facing gardens and borders can still grow many vegetables well and some fruit, and will provide better conditions for many foliage plants, especially in a dry summer.

The need to differentiate between east and west is less obvious, but facing east can be a problem for some plants; exposure to the rising sun can be fatal to frosted blossoms. Worse still can be exposure to icy blasts from winds at inopportune times such as during fruit blossom. Facing into the prevailing winds (southwest in the UK) also brings more rain and such areas are not suitable for plants that like to be warm, dry and sheltered. In addition, it is important to think about your own enjoyment of the garden: plants that flower best in the morning or the evening should be placed where you can get the best of them for most appreciation, and a summerhouse or seat should face west because it is more likely to be used in the evening.

Micro-climate

Every garden has its own micro-climate and smaller ones within it. Because of many factors, particularly the aspect of the site as a whole, the amount of shade from surroundings, the shape and nature of the walls and fences, the heat escaping from homes and drains and the pooling of cold air down slopes creating frost pockets, each and every spot is slightly different. Although you may enjoy much the same conditions as others in your street, your garden has within it spots that at different times of year and day are much more favourable to some plant or another. It is also within our power to improve these spots much further, which in temperate climates usually means increasing shelter from the wind and capturing more sun. In sunnier climes, however, providing shade is as important for many plants.

> One gardener's sunny wall is another's shady one

Below: This mixed border shows shasta daisies, bergamot and phlox blooming in midsummer, while trees and other perennials provide structure during the winter months.

Disease-resistant plants

In many ways the plants we grow have been selected because they are inherently trouble-free, but few cultivars are immune to all pests and diseases. The more important crops are grown most frequently, and thus have acquired the most pests and diseases to bother them.

For these economically important crops, which include some popular ornamentals, much research has been done to find varieties resistant to the common ailments. Most success has been against diseases, especially with those of vegetable crops. Also, roses have long been bred with considerable mildew and black spot resistance.

> Pests are harder to discourage as the hungry critters want their lunch

Pests are harder to discourage as the hungry critters want their lunch. However, by changing the smell and colour, the pest can sometimes be confused. Unfortunately, after a time, resistant plants start to fail as the pests and the diseases alter and start to attack again. However, for the most important crops new varieties are continually being introduced, which makes recommending any one variety pointless. Because of all the effort which is made is into securing the crop, little attention is paid to cooking and eating qualities. So a small drawback in choosing resistant varieties is that this inevitably entails some loss of flavour or quality in comparison with other varieties. Thus it is a good idea to grow at least a couple of sorts with one for reliability and another for flavour.

Above: The 'Muscat Hamburg' vine.

Above: The yellow tomato variety 'Golden Sunrise'.

Crops with some resistance

Crop	Diseases and pests	Crop	Diseases and pests
Asparagus	Botrytis	Onions	Downy mildew Botrytis White rot
Beans	Mosaic virus Anthracnose Halo blight	Parsnips	Canker
Blackcurrants	Mildew	Peas	Powdery mildew Common wilt Downy mildew Enation virus *Fusarium* wilt
Brussels sprouts	Leaf spot Powdery mildew		
Calabrese/ broccoli	Black rot Downy mildew Clubroot	Peppers	Tobacco mosaic virus
		Potatoes	Blight Golden eelworms Scab Blackleg Gangrene White eelworms Leaf roll
Carrots	Root flies		
Courgettes and marrows	Cucumber mosaic virus Powdery mildew		
Cucumbers	Cucumber mosaic virus Powdery mildew Scab Leaf spot *Cladosporium* leaf mould		
		Raspberries	Aphids
		Spinach	Mildew
Gooseberries	Mildew	Swedes	Clubroot Mildew
Grapes	Downy mildew Powdery mildew		
		Sweetcorn	Rust
Leeks	Rust	Tomatoes	Tobacco mosaic virus *Fusarium* wilt *Cladosporium* leaf mould *Verticillium* wilt Mildew
Lettuces	Root aphids Mosaic virus Mildew Aphids		
Melons	Powdery mildew *Fusarium* wilt		

Companion planting

Companion planting is usually associated with vegetable growing, and it refers to the crops that can be combined successfully and give added benefits over simple intercropping.

Care must be taken not to crowd plants, but as long as sufficient air, light, nutrients and water are available some combinations of crops do particularly well together. For example, instead of three beds growing, respectively, peas, potatoes and sweetcorn, I find that growing all three crops on the three beds gives a higher total yield. On each bed I grow peas in a narrow row down the centre and flank the row on either side with alternate sweetcorn and potato plants. The peas provide shelter for the other young shoots, the potatoes keep the soil covered and moist, which the sweetcorn and peas enjoy, and none shades out the others.

> Combining and mixing crops significantly reduces damage from pests and diseases

In addition, combining and mixing crops significantly reduces the damage from pests and diseases. For example, I have found that beetroot grown between swedes and parsnips do not get attacked by the birds.

Helpful herbs

• Many annual herbs are beneficial when they are grown with crops, especially as their strong scents help to hide the food plants from their pests.
• Perennial herbs, such as rosemary, thyme, sage, chives, southernwood, hyssop and lavender, are beneficial around the edges of the vegetable plot, where their scents are effective pest-deterrents and their flowers bring in predators for the pests and pollinators for the crops.
• Most useful of all are French marigolds, which should be planted in every plot and by paths and gates so you brush against them, releasing their pungent smell.
• In the fruit garden, companion plants will compete initially but later can be of immense benefit in attracting and maintaining predators and pollinators. *Limnanthes douglasii* (poached-egg plant), *Convolvulus tricolor*, chives, nasturtiums, rosemary, thyme and sage will all be of benefit, and clovers and alfalfa can be added to the grass-seed mixture when grassing down trees.

Sacrifical crops

Some plants are grown to attract pests away from the main planting. They may be the same plant grown around the edge of the plot or a more attractive lure. For example, redcurrants will keep birds off the blackcurrants. In the same way, if you shred surplus leaves or seedlings when transplanting and spread the mixture around the transplants, it will fob off slugs.

Trap plants are similar to sacrificials. For example, sweet tobaccos, especially *Nicotiana sylvestris*, have sticky stems and leaves and are attractive to whiteflies and thrips. Growing these among other plants draws pests, which can then be further 'stuck on' with a sugar solution spray and removed with the plant.

Companion planting: vegetables

Vegetable	Does well with	Does badly with
Beans, broad	Brassicas, carrots, celery, cucurbits, potatoes, summer savory and most herbs	Garlic and onions
Beans, French	Celery, cucurbits, potatoes, strawberries and sweetcorn	Garlic and onions
Beans, runner	Sweetcorn and summer savory	Beetroot and chards
Beetroot and chards	Beans (most), brassicas, garlic, kohl rabi, onions, parsnips and swedes	Runner beans
Brassicas and cabbage family	Beetroot, celery, chards, dill, garlic, nasturtiums, onions, peas and tomatoes	Runner beans and strawberries
Carrots	Chives, garlic, leeks, lettuces, onions, peas and tomatoes	
Celery and celeriac	Brassicas, beans, leeks and tomatoes	
Cucurbits (cucumber, courgette, marrow, melon, pumpkin and squash)	Beans, nasturtiums, peas and sweetcorn	Potatoes
Garlic and onions	Beetroot, chards, lettuces, strawberries, summer savory and tomatoes	Beans and peas
Leeks	Carrots, celery and onions	
Lettuces	Carrots, chervil, cucurbits, radishes and strawberries	
Peas	Beans, carrots, curcubits, sweetcorn and turnips	Garlic and onions
Potatoes	Beans, brassicas, peas and sweetcorn	Cucurbits and tomatoes
Swedes and turnips	Peas	
Sweetcorn	Beans, curcubits, peas and potatoes	
Tomatoes	Asparagus, basil, carrots, garlic, onions and parsley	Kohl rabi and potatoes

'Beneficial' and companion plants

Mixtures of plants are less bothered by pests than monocultures, but we can also use companions, such as aromatic herbs, deliberately to camouflage or disguise the scent of the crop. French marigolds are particularly effective; they not only hide other plants but actually discourage and poison pests. They discourage whiteflies from coming into the greenhouse and kill nematodes in the soil. (In the USA gardeners grow old-fashioned varieties as modern French marigolds have been bred to have less smell!) I use golden feverfew for its strong scent and cheerful appearance. Most of the daisy family, Compositae, seem helpful in this way as well as being pretty, and they are almost all attractive to beneficial insects. The edible chrysanthemum 'Shungi-ku', is also a pungent and effective companion, keeping many pests off brassicas and related ornamentals. Almost as useful as the French marigolds are the African and Mexican forms, though these grow much bigger.

Chives and garlic are renowned as good companions for most plants. *Limnanthes douglasii*, *Phacelia tanacetifolia*, pot marigold, *Convolvolus tricolor* and alpine strawberries are all excellent companions for bringing in beneficial

Above: Nasturtiums are cheerful, attractive and edible plants with beneficial effects.

insects and some should be grown in every area. Nasturtiums are always reckoned to drive woolly aphids off apple trees and this applies to all the ornamental forms as well. Lavender under roses is a traditional companion to keep their pests away. I also find catnip works well and dies down in winter allowing the addition of thicker mulches.

Companion plants and disease prevention

Many gardeners believe that some companion plants, such as nettles and alliums, actually help prevent fungal and bacterial attacks on other plants. Although not many of us want stinging nettles all over the garden they can be allowed in moderation in wild gardens, and they are quite good to eat when young. However, there are many

> Nasturtiums are always reckoned to drive woolly aphids off apple trees

prettier deadnettle relatives that are also good companions, flowering over a long period and much more suited to ornamental areas.

Chives and garlic are traditionally grown under roses, fruit and ornamentals to discourage fungal and bacterial diseases, and as they are strong accumulators of sulphur there may be reason. There are many ornamental alliums that probably have similar properties and would look better – though there is little to match the flowering heads of leeks! Camomile is said to be the plant physician and aids other plants growing nearby – anyway it smells good and makes a calming tea.

Below: An underplanting of Limnanthes douglasii *maintains a healthy supply of predators and pollinators in the fruit cage.*

Companion planting in ornamental areas

Most of the good companions, such as French marigolds and aromatic herbs, that benefit fruit and vegetables also suit ornamentals. So, when planning ornamental areas of shrubs and trees, include some of those along with some evergreen shrubs and dense groundcover to give shelter and nest sites all year round. Plant deep- and shallow-rooters and include several leguminous species such as *Acacia, Cercis, Genista, Gleditsia, Spartium* and *Cytisus*.

Likewise among herbaceous plants include a few dense evergreen clumps and mix in leguminous plants such as lupins, *Galega, Baptisia, Hedysarum* and sweet peas.

Basic plant care

Good methods and conditions set plants off with a flying start and keep them growing without check or hindrance. Plants that are once checked or slowed down in their growth never do as well as those that grow consistently: their tissues harden and further growth is restrained.

In many ways growing plants is a bit like looking after babies. It is critical to get them through the earliest stages, but later on they are tough enough to endure less careful treatment with little risk of permanent damage. So organic gardeners ensure freedom from early stress, and keep down the competition from weeds and other plants. This treatment produces healthy, robust plants which grow well in spite of attacks from pests and diseases, in much the same way as humans shrug off colds and scratches.

Rotation

In the vegetable garden rotation is the most important technique (see page 82). Move the plant each year, and pests and diseases overwintering in the soil emerge to find their target has gone. The same applies to replanting and disease: never replace a dead shrubby plant with another of the same.

> In many ways growing plants is a bit like looking after babies

Rotation also changes and modifies the conditions in the soil, ensuring that fewer pests or disease spores survive until the crop returns.

Timing

Plants that are grown in season are the healthiest and survive most diseases, but there can be an advantage in early or late sowing if the crop thereby misses the worst attacks of a pest or disease. In most years, for example, early potatoes are out of the ground before blight becomes a problem. Overwintered broad beans are usually too tough early in the season for black aphids to bother them. Likewise, early-sown carrots miss root flies, especially if they are harvested early, and late-sown ones may also avoid the pest at the end of the season.

Pests and diseases

Indoor or undercover propagation not only helps to give plants a better early or late start and so help them to escape attacks, but can also prevent these entirely by isolating the crop during its most vulnerable stage. Beetroot sown in the open can be razed to the ground by birds but may survive if planted out when they are bigger.

Accurate sowing and indoor propagation also overcome the need for thinning, which can attract pests by spreading the plants' scent, as happens with carrot flies or onion flies.

Summer pruning of shrubby plants is beneficial because it controls growth and so encourages flowering and fruiting. It can simultaneously remove a developing pest population, especially aphids, as these cluster on tips. During the winter months rake aside heavy mulches put down in autumn. This will disturb many pests, which may be hibernating, and they will be either killed directly or through exposure to birds. This is especially useful against gooseberry sawflies and raspberry beetles. A heavy mulch applied before regrowth in spring seals spores and infective material beneath it. This is recommended for most plants, and is particularly effective against an attack of black spot on roses.

Seaweed sprays

These are applied to boost growth and are also good for reducing pest and disease problems. They do not act directly as pesticides but aid the plants to make resilient, vigorous growth that throws off attacks. The smell of seaweed may also help by confusing pests.

Above: The rose 'Zéphirine Drouhin' climbs up to meet the trailing vine, creating a shady area.

Below: This grass path works well with the dense leylandii hedge and acid-green feverfew border to create an enticing alleyway.

Watering

More plants do badly through over- or underwatering than from almost all other causes together. In times of strong growth it is almost impossible to overwater plants in the open ground. Plants growing in pots in winter can be difficult to underwater. It is between these two extremes that the difficulty lies.

In the open ground try to conserve winter rains with mulches and except during droughts restrict watering to: before sowing; newly emergent seedlings; new transplants; and crops at a critical stage (usually when their flowers are setting). In times of drought, water the most valued plants with one long soak rather than everything little and often, as much of this will just evaporate. Above all, keep down weed competition and mulch well.

Do not try to wet large areas of soil around each plant as this mostly evaporates. Instead, try to soak water down to the roots. A whole, half-

> In times of drought, water the most valued plants with one long soak

Below: Thyme enjoys a position that provides warmth at ground level combined with a cool root run.

Drought-resistent plants

As the climate dries and we economize on water, we need to grow fewer water-demanding plants. Rather than planting out displays of bedding plants, permanent evergreen ground cover makes more sense and the days of the lawn seem numbered. Obviously plants adapted to a Mediterranean or desert climate are mostly well suited to a no- or low-watering regime, but you could also consider those native to dry sandy soils such as the heaths and seaside plants. Herbs, especially those with silvery or grey aromatic foliage, thrive in dry, sunny conditions. Among crop plants there are few that do really well on dry soil, but perennial and deep-rooted crops, such as some fruit trees, do better than vegetables, especially figs and grapes if they are well established initially.

buried pot, or a trench beside plants that need copious watering, speeds up the task. A neat idea is to take a clear plastic bottle with the bottom cut off (this can be used as a mini-cloche elsewhere). Invert the top and push it in beside a plant; a litre or two can then be poured rapidly into the funnel to trickle in slowly. A pair of watering cans with sawn-off spouts are easily carried and pour faster than those with roses or long narrow spouts (but always use a rose when watering directly onto the soil surface).

Rainwater is usually preferable to tapwater, because it is warmer coming from a butt than up out of the mains, and it has fewer minerals, with no chlorine or fluoride added. However, rainwater is not sterile and it can cause damping off of young seedlings.

Automatic watering systems

These can be as simple as a slowly filling, self-emptying cistern, a constant drip from a network of pipes, underground porous pipes or direct feeds, or as complicated as a misting or spraying system all controlled by a timer, electrically or even by computerized remote sensors. They are quite expensive to set up and difficult to get right initially but then save a lot of time, and are of most use where the same things are being grown all the time. A simple trick for the odd plant is to stand a big container of water higher than the pot and lead a wick of a wetted, rolled up piece of cloth from the reservoir down to the compost.

Right: This water butt is made from a recycled deep freeze, which has been painted matt black.

You can increase your water-holding capacity by linking several butts with syphons. One butt on the patio by a downpipe can fill up half-a-dozen behind the shed and one in the greenhouse and another on the vegetable bed. The butts need to be adjusted to the same level, so that when you take water out of any one all the others fill it up again. This means that you do not need to carry water around the garden as much: it is waiting for you.

Step 5 Encourage wildlife

Organic gardeners want as many types of wildlife as possible. The more forms of life, the more they control each other and the more fertilizer rains down on our crops. Not only that but they are interesting and beautiful to observe. Moreover if we encourage small things then bigger ones survive. I'm sorry for the blackbird taken by the hawk but it was fantastic to see – and only the summer before I saw a blackbird eat a newt!

How to attract wildlife

It is easy to provide wildlife with a wide variety of food – it is called a garden; but our overtidiness in the garden has eliminated too many of the nooks and crannies where wildlife lives and, as with birds' nests, we need artificial alternatives. Obviously a dovecote needs to be decorative as well as functional, but on the smaller scale our provision for birds can be very humble and of recycled materials as the nests are so small and easily hidden.

The smallest creatures hibernate inside dry bundles of sticks and under piles of stones. Water and damp places are essential for others; a pile of rotting logs beside a pool, for example, will attract beetles to lay their eggs.

Above: Foxgloves and an old rotting log provide shelter for wildlife and an attractive wild corner.

Water in the garden

Water in any form will give a lot of pleasure and is almost essential in an organic garden: even a tiny pond adds to the atmosphere and is also wonderfully attractive to wildlife. Birds, insects and animals all need water and will come to your garden if you supply it; once there, they help with pest control. Also, if water is more accessible, birds eat less fruit. A bird bath can be fitted into every garden – ideally where it can be seen from a window and is safe from cats. A fountain or cascade, however humble, is a delight and can be combined with a pond (though waterlilies like still water). Ponds do not have to be large to attract wildlife, provided they never dry up. Even an old bath set in the ground will do well. All water

Above: The honey-scented Buddleja globosa *is good for attracting insects.*

needs a sloping edge to let creatures in and out, and secure fencing if young children are around.

In a large garden you could have ponds in different areas to make different ecosystems. Large ponds create micro-climates that can shelter tender plants nearby, and they reflect sunlight onto surrounding plants as well as providing an emergency source of water.

When making a pond, line it with newspaper and old carpet first to prevent the liner being punctured on stones. Similarly lay old carpet upside down over the edges to protect the liner from light and wear, so that it lasts longer. Butyl rubber is the best value as it lasts longer, but the cheaper alternatives are just as good if well protected.

> Ponds do not have to be large to attract wildlife

Fill the pond and let it stand for a week to warm up and lose chlorine before stocking it. Take a bucket to a 'natural' pond and scoop up some mud and water for an instant ecosystem.

Above: A pond is important in an organic garden because it provides a habitat for lots of wildlife.

Nooks, crannies, hedges and hedgehogs

As well as providing food, it is well worth adding places for beneficial animals to rest, hibernate or lay eggs. If you think about the natural sites they prefer, it will give you ideas about what to add.

Hidey-holes

Frogs, newts and toads are encouraged primarily by a pool or pond but they also spend much of their lives on land. In the winter they want damp, frost-free places, ideally damp burrows beside a pond that are well insulated from above and just above the highest floodline! These can easily be created with old drainage pipes, bricks and stones and covered with a layer of soil and turf.

Piles of decaying logs and bark provide a multitude of resources and are especially useful as low walls around ponds where they also prevent children and herons gaining easy access. Such piles may be accused of harbouring pests and diseases such as honey fungus. However, I have never seen evidence of a pile initiating such an attack, while freshly killed tree stumps have often. Piles of stones, bricks, tiles and even bottles are all useful to many small creatures for nest and hibernation sites and these can be hidden under hedges and large shrubs. (Bottles must be positioned neck down or filled with sticks or they are deadfall traps.) Even piles of sand left undisturbed soon get colonized by many interesting insects, and creating a sandy or chalky bank will bring in some rarities.

Hedges, especially dense and evergreen ones, provide lots of niches for creatures to live in. Mixed informal hedges provide variety but a neat formal hedge has a dry internal space that can be filled with nest and hibernation sites. The ground underneath can be thickly mulched with the hedge's own prunings, in most cases with little risk of disease, and this attracts many creatures.

Lacewing hotels and ladybird refuges

These most important pollinators and predators can both be helped by providing them with winter quarters. You can make your own out of bundles of hollow stems. These can be simply tied, or made more weatherproof by inserting them in a tube cut from a plastic bottle, then hidden out of sight inside dense and evergreen shrubs, trees and hedges. Even bundles of thorny prunings can be utilized this way to make snug refuges.

Hedgehogs

These wonderful slug-eaters need somewhere dry where they can hibernate undisturbed. A wooden box about 45–60cm (18–24in) square is ideal, but a cardboard box may do if well insulated and put under the floor of a garden shed. Provide an entrance and a bowl of water. Hedgehogs should not be given bread and milk as it is not good for them; cat and dog food or pilchards are better.

Attracting beneficial insects

Building up self-regulating ecosystems means making good provision for predators – incorporating plants to provide nectar, fruits and pollen; shelter on the large and small scale; sites for nests and hibernation quarters; an accessible and reliable water supply; and sacrificial plants to breed up pests on which the predators and parasites can be maintained.

Companion plants that encourage predators should ideally keep flowering throughout the whole season and particularly early on in the year. Not all flowers are equally useful though: deep-throated flowers intended for moths and butterflies, and double flowers which have been specially bred for their beauty at the cost of nectar, are less effective.

Of all beneficial insects, hoverflies are probably the most important, and they are attracted to *Limnanthes douglasii* (poached-egg plant) in particular. This can be grown as a self-seeding annual under roses, shrubs and fruit. Ladybirds, lacewings and predatory wasps are attracted to the same flowers as hoverflies but also like alliums, anthemis, fennel and yarrow. Aphids will seek out patches of nettles, honeysuckles, sweet cherries and lupins, which then maintain a background level of predators and parasites.

> Double flowers specially bred for their beauty at the cost of nectar are less effective

Above: Buddleja is worth growing for the beautiful Peacock butterflies it attracts.

Below: The aphids on this foxglove appear to be doing no harm and are distracted from plants that they might really damage.

Attracting beneficial insects

Plants for insects and wildlife

Plant	Animals attracted					
	Hover-flies	Bees	Lady-birds	Lace-wings	Butter-flies	Birds
Achillea millefolium (yarrow)	✓	✓	✓	✓		
Ajuga reptans (bugle)		✓				
Allium schoenoprasum (chives)		✓				
Anchusa azurea (alkanet)		✓				
Anethum graveolens (dill)	✓					
Angelica archangelica (angelica)	✓					
Anthemis				✓		
Arabis caucasica (rockcress)		✓				
Bergenia	✓					
Borago officinalis (borage)		✓				
Buddleja davidii				✓	✓	
Calendula (marigold)	✓		✓			
Campanula		✓				
Centaurea	✓					
Centranthus ruber (valerian)		✓			✓	
Chrysanthemum (shasta daisy)	✓					
Convolvulus tricolor	✓			✓		
Coreopsis grandiflora (tickweed)		✓				
Cosmos	✓	✓		✓		
Delphinium		✓				
Digitalis (foxglove)		✓				
Dipsacus fullonum (teasel)		✓			✓	✓
Echinops ritro		✓				
Eryngium (sea holly)		✓				
Erysimum (wallflowers)		✓				
Eschscholzia californica		✓				
Filipendula ulmaria (meadowsweet)						✓
Foeniculum vulgare (fennel)	✓	✓	✓			
Geranium (cranesbill)						✓
Gypsophila (baby's breath)		✓			✓	
Helianthus (sunflower)		✓			✓	✓
Heliotropium arborescens (cherry pie)					✓	
Hyssopus officinalis (hyssop)		✓				

Plants for insects and wildlife

Plant	Animals attracted					
	Hover-flies	Bees	Lady-birds	Lace-wings	Butter-flies	Birds
Iberis (candytuft)					✓	
Lamium album (deadnettle)		✓				
Lavandula (lavender)		✓				
Lavatera (mallow)		✓				
Levisticum officinale (lovage)	✓					
Limnanthes douglasii (poached-egg plant)	✓	✓				
Lobularia maritima (alyssum)		✓			✓	
Lonicera (honeysuckle)		✓			✓	
Lunaria biennis (honesty)					✓	✓
Lysimachia punctata (yellow loosestrife)		✓				
Melissa officinalis (balm)						
Mentha (mint)		✓			✓	
Monarda didyma		✓			✓	
Muscari (grape hyacinth)		✓				
Myosotis (forget-me-not)		✓				
Myrrhis odorata	✓					
Nepeta (catmint)		✓			✓	
Origanum vulgare (marjoram)		✓			✓	
Papaver officinale (poppy)		✓				
Phacelia tanacetifolia	✓	✓				
Pyracantha (firethorn)						✓
Reseda odorata (mignonette)		✓			✓	
Ribes (flowering currant)		✓				
Rosmarinus officinalis (rosemary)		✓				
Rudbeckia	✓					
Saponaria officinalis (soapwort)					✓	
Sedum spectabile (ice plant)		✓			✓	
Solidago (goldenrod)	✓	✓		✓		
Symphytum officinale (comfrey)		✓				
Tagetes (marigold)	✓					
Thymus (thyme)		✓				
Trifolium (clover)		✓				

Encouraging beneficial birds

Birds are most easily increased by the provision of nesting boxes as suitable sites are now rare. It is important to encourage the most useful birds: blue tits, great tits, tree sparrows and other small insectivorous birds need little wooden boxes about 13–15cm (5–6in) all round with a hole at the front of 4cm (1³⁄₄in). Robins, wagtails and flycatchers prefer the box to have a bigger opening, of 5 x 7.5cm (2 x 3in). These resemble natural nesting holes and should be fixed to trees where cats and other predators cannot get at them. Put them where you can watch from a window, except those for robins, which like boxes to be well hidden away in shrubs or hedges. Many other birds, such as blackbirds and thrushes, find ample nest sites in dense evergreens or thick hedges. You can also encourage birds by providing a supply of water, feeding them kitchen scraps or wild bird seed on a bird table, and fitting berry-carrying shrubs into the garden.

Food for birds

The simplest way to provide food for birds is, of course, to put out peanuts (make sure they are aflatoxin-free) and wild bird seed. When you are designing your garden, it is worth thinking about where such items as bird tables and bird baths will be positioned. This is not a problem with free-standing ones, but if you want a suspended bird table you will have to give the siting more thought. From the birds' point of view, it does not much matter where the feeding station is, as long as it is safe from surprise attacks from cats or dogs. If you want to enjoy watching birds as they feed, consider placing the bird table where it can be seen easily from a window.

Berries and seeds represent the major part of many birds' diets, and these can be provided by including shrubs and other plants that bear berries in the garden. Small trees, including *Sorbus* (rowan) and *Ilex aquifolium* (holly), bear berries that are greatly enjoyed by birds in winter. Perennial plants are also a useful source of seeds. Many birds, notably goldfinches, will visit gardens in large numbers to feed on seedheads that have been left. Leaving old vegetation standing throughout winter can make a garden look rather unkempt and untidy, but it is worth leaving at least some through the cold months. The old vegetation is a hiding place for many insects, and insectivorous birds will come seeking food.

Below: The handsome red berries of Berberis thunbergii *attract fieldfares and redwings.*

Trees and shrubs for berries

Plant	Features
Berberis thunbergii (barberry)	A deciduous shrub with bright red berries in winter for thrushes, including fieldfares and redwings
Cotoneaster horizontalis	Red winter berries attract thrushes of all kinds and waxwings
Crataegus monogyna (common hawthorn)	Glossy, dark red berries provide food for many species in winter, including starlings, finches, crows, blue tits, thrushes and waxwings
Hedera helix (ivy)	Autumn and winter berries are an important food for wood pigeons, collared doves, waxwings, thrushes, jays, starlings and finches
Ilex aquifolium (common holly)	The red autumn and winter berries are especially appreciated by mistle thrushes
Leycesteria formosa (Himalayan honeysuckle)	In autumn red-purple berries attract tits, thrushes, finches and warblers
Lonicera periclymenum (honeysuckle)	Glossy red autumn berries are enjoyed by robins, blackbirds, song thrushes, garden warblers, tits, crows, finches and waxwings
Pyracantha 'Orange Glow'	Vivid orange fruits in autumn to winter are enjoyed by wood pigeons and thrushes
Sambucus racemosa (red-berried elder)	Waxwings and thrushes will eat the autumn fruits
Sorbus aria (whitebeam)	The colourful autumn berries are a valuable food for wood pigeons, fieldfares, redwings, blackbirds and mistle thrushes

Grow organic

Vegetables and fruit need the best possible conditions, which means growing them in a deep, rich soil that has been well fed with organic material. If the soil is poor, you will have to do a great deal of work before it is worthwhile even trying to grow food crops.

The vegetable plot

Ideally, the area should be in full sun, with no overhanging trees. Wet, boggy sites and low ground should be avoided, as they will result in winter losses and frost damage in spring. The plot should not be too far from the kitchen, a water source and the garden shed, or much time will be wasted going to and fro.

Crop rotation

It is critical is that you do not grow the same crop, or a near relation, on the same piece of ground year after year. Move the crop around or leave it out entirely for a year or two. What follows what is not that important, although some combinations can be less satisfactory – potatoes do not happily follow brassicas or

legumes if the soil was limed for them, for example – but it is important to make sure that you do not replant potatoes, tomatoes and brassicas in the same spot for as many years as possible, and that other vegetables are not grown on the same site as the year before.

Of course, the more elaborate your rotation and the longer the gaps, the better the results, and this is easier if you grow a wider variety of crops in smaller amounts, and if you introduce 'break crops', such as flowers, strawberries or artichokes, to the plot for a few years.

Row or block planting

Block and row planting are alternative ways of laying out crops. Those that need support, such as peas, are better in rows that run north–south, so that the ground between is not shaded. Rows are not essential, however: you can even grow beans and peas in a circle by attaching a wheel to the top of a pole and running strings down from it. Rows waste a lot of space and the paths between them get compacted and need digging. For most crops, especially those that are close planted, such as carrots, block planting is better. Apart from saving space and reducing digging, it helps with weed control, because once the plants are half-grown their foliage meets, excluding light from the soil and choking out weed seedlings. This also forms a favourable micro-climate and prevents moisture loss. If netting or fleece is used to prevent pests reaching the plants, block planting is again more practical. For successful block planting you need loose, deep soil to enable the roots to go deeper in search of nutrients.

Raised beds

Many of the advantages of raised beds come from their being fixed. They are simply permanent sub-plots surrounded by narrow paths. The beds are not walked on, so need digging only every seven or eight years, and they make block planting easy, although rows can still be run down the middle if the beds run north–south. The ideal width is about 1.2m (4ft), which is comfortable to reach from either side, and they should be no longer than about 5m (16ft), or you will be tempted to walk over rather than around them. Having permanently fixed beds makes record-keeping and thus crop rotation a simple process.

Fixed beds slowly become raised beds naturally as mulches, compost and root residues build up.

As well as making them less back-breaking to work, raising the soil level has several advantages. As the bed builds up, the surface area increases, not only giving some extra planting space but also increasing aeration and evaporation. They give an earlier start in spring because the soil warms up sooner; and in winter the crops on top are in slightly warmer conditions as cold air runs off to lower levels. However, raised beds also dry out more quickly in summer, and mulches tend to slide off or be pulled off by birds.

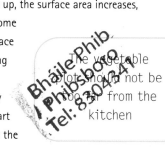

On the whole, the advantages outweigh the problems, especially if their shape is kept to the natural curve formed by the soil. This provides several useful micro-climates. In a bed running north–south, the sunny end is a hot slope, suitable for early cropping and tender herbs, while the shaded end suits salad and leaf crops. The sides are protected from the wind and thus stay moist, suiting leeks, roots and salad crops. The top is open ground, but especially well suited to onions, shallots, brassicas and legumes grown in rows and for overwintering vegetables.

Paths of compacted soil are sufficient but get muddy in the wet. Sharp sand or crushed gravel is more suitable and it doesn't matter if some gets mixed into the soil.

Raising beds artificially with planks, bricks or a similar material around the sides reduces the area available for planting, removes many of the useful micro-climates, adds to costs and provides hiding places for pests.

Growing in a greenhouse

A greenhouse is a great boon for raising plants and extending the growing season. Greenhouses come in sizes to suit most pockets and gardens, and are worthwhile as an aid to gardening, but they can take up a lot of time and money if you fill them with tender plants in pots. The smaller the garden, the more valuable greenhouse space will be, as it enables you to start off plants for later planting as beds become vacant.

A greenhouse needs to be near the house for access and services but is also difficult to site attractively because screening may rob it of light. In many ways a conservatory may be a more practical solution and saves siting a greenhouse within view of the house. Water nearby is essential, and electric light and power will allow evening work and the use of thermostatic propagation, further increasing the value of the greenhouse. Wooden greenhouses are slightly easier on the eye than metal-framed ones and tend to be warmer. Extra plastic insulation is a mixed blessing, because although it keeps greenhouses warmer it reduces the light. Ventilation must be adequate and automatic, unless you are at home all day.

Organic management under cover

Growing under walk-in cover, whether in the form of a greenhouse or polytunnel, is an artificial method of gardening, and it requires more intervention because the natural systems cannot control pests and diseases, the temperature may rise too far, and rain does not fall.

There are two main approaches:

1. A 'sterile environment' approach involves cleaning the greenhouse thoroughly, using a high-pressure water or steam jet, and treating the plants only if they are subject to any attack using some of the methods described on pages 31 and 33. This method resembles the conventional approach to gardening.

Polytunnels

Polytunnels are less visually appealing than greenhouses, but they are ideal for a large garden because they give a lot of space for the money and are easy to move. They need to be well ventilated, as they are prone to high humidity which can promote fungal diseases. The cover will need replacing every four years or so, when the tunnel can be moved to a different piece of ground – the vegetable bed is convenient because it can then be incorporated into the crop rotation.

2. The alternative is to try to build up semi-natural systems, concentrating more on using predators for pest control.
• Water in saucers, nests of straw-filled pots and groundcover plants can be included under staging and in shady corners for beetles, frogs and toads.
• Ladybirds, spiders and bought-in predators, such as those outlined on page 33, can be introduced

Above: The external appearance of the polytunnel is much improved by growing climbers and lush herbs immediately outside.

Below: Nicotiana sylvestris *has sticky leaves which trap any whiteflies and thrips that the marigolds at the entrance fail to discourage.*

and encouraged with rolled-up cardboard nests tied in dry nooks and crannies. With this approach, even organic pesticides cannot be used, because the natural predators will suffer, but companion plants can be used. It is beneficial to grow French marigolds in the greenhouse or polytunnel, especially by the door where you brush against them and release their scent, because they keep out whiteflies but attract bees and hoverflies. *Nicotiana* (sweet tobacco plant) and *Nicotiana sylvestris* (wild tobacco plant) are also beneficial because their sticky stems trap many little insects, such as thrips.

It is preferable to grow plants to fruition directly in the soil rather than in containers, because it saves on watering and compost. Even with rotation, moving the plants around each year and adding copious amounts of garden compost, however, yields start to drop after five years or so. The answer is simply to dig out the topsoil and replace it with compost and fresh soil dug from a clean part of the garden. This is hard work but does not need doing often and is less work than filling up and watering loads of containers every year.

> Remember that fruit grown under cover will need pollinating by hand

Old carpet and cardboard can be used to cover bare soil in greenhouses and polytunnels and makes rather effective paths. This prevents weeds germinating and minimizes moisture loss, stops splashing of soil onto crops, is more pleasant to work on, and when the strips are rolled back makes it easy to pick off slugs and other pests hiding there.

Vegetables

A greenhouse is not needed for starting off hardy vegetables in cells or pots as they will be more than happy in a coldframe or sheltered spot until they are ready to go out. However, a greenhouse does make it easier to provide better conditions earlier, especially enough light and warmth, and this can then be used later for growing tender crops to fruition. Cloches are nearly as good but do not have as much space and are difficult to use, and while polytunnels give the best value for money they are not nice to look at. Whatever you choose, be careful to keep the glass or plastic clean, as light is more important than heat for most plants, especially hardy vegetables. Ventilation is also important as it is easy to cook small seedlings if the full sun comes out on them while they are tightly sealed up – either be vigilant or invest in an automatic vent opener.

Once hardy vegetables have started growing well in pots, then they can be planted out into the main plot, but they must be hardened off first. This simply means getting them used to tougher

Greenhouse hygiene

Common greenhouse diseases are mildew, blight, botrytis and leaf spot (see pages 44–9). In general, they can be controlled by maintaining strict hygiene in the greenhouse, and any diseased or damaged plants should be removed immediately. Good ventilation is essential to prevent plants suffering from moisture or heat stress.

conditions by standing them outside each day, but putting them back under cover at night for three or four days. Do not skimp on this important exercise unless cloches or clear plastic bottles are used to protect plants when they are first put outside, in which case they can be planted out with a little less initial hardening off.

Fruit

In colder regions tender crops, including tropical fruit, can be grown in the greenhouse. This gives excellent bird and frost protection and earlier crops, but on the down side tends to cause more pest and disease problems. There is no background ecology of predators and parasites, and diseases tend to spread more easily in the close, often humid conditions inside.

To combat pests try companion planting of flowers, such as *Tagetes* (French marigolds), which attract aphid predators. Alternatively, spray with soft soap or use biological pest control of whiteflies and red spider mites by introducing parasites (see page 33).

Right: The large plant in the doorway is the shoo-fly plant (Nicandra physaloides) *which discourages whiteflies from attacking valuable food crops.*

Fruits can be grown either in border soil or in containers in a greenhouse. The advantage of using containers in the greenhouse is that this restricts growth more easily than pruning. It also enables plants to be stood outside for the summer months, but they will then require even more careful watering. Container growing in a greenhouse is most suitable for grapes, peaches and citrus fruits. Remember that fruit grown under cover will need pollinating by hand.

Growing in containers

One advantage of containers is that you are free to choose a potting compost to suit the plants you wish to grow. Ordinary soil is too poor for most plants confined in a pot and a strong loam-based compost such as John Innes potting should be used. Peat-based composts (see pages 12–13) are really too light for containers and the best substitute is a loam-based compost (except for ericaceous plants). This can be mixed with other ingredients such as leafmould and rotted turves for really large containers but do not economize when filling small pots; plants need good stuff if they are to do well. I use sieved garden compost for potting most subjects and always for the bigger and tougher plants.

Do not mulch plants in pots as it stops the soil breathing, though a thin layer of sharp sand or gravel suppresses weeds and reduces splashing. Plants in containers need careful feeding with well-diluted liquid feeds and perennials also need top dressing and repotting every year or so. Be diligent with regular watering otherwise they'll do badly, and conversely be careful not to let their drainage become poor and drown them.

> Do not mulch plants in pots as it stops the soil breathing

Vegetables and herbs

It is possible to grow almost any vegetable in a suitable container but it has to be very deep for root vegetables such as maincrop carrots and parsnips, and some crops such as maincrop potatoes are hardly worth the space. However, choice favourites are worth having and given enough sun, soil and water can be grown. The smaller plants are obviously easier.

Good choices
• Radishes, spring onions, shallots, onions, garlic, lettuces, beetroot and French beans are all very straightforward container subjects.
• Short, stumpy sorts of carrots are generally more successful than larger ones.
• Climbers and ramblers such as gherkins, gourds, cucumbers and runner beans can be grown if they are kept well watered.
• Herbs are particularly appropriate for containers as they are mostly small and are used in small amounts yet are expensive to buy. Moreover, most can be taken indoors for the cold months and kept on a sunny windowsill.

Fruit

In the smallest gardens it is still possible to grow fruit trees, soft fruit and even vines, by confining them in containers. This cramps the root system, preventing them from getting too big, and tends to bring them into fruit earlier and means that much less pruning is required than for soil-grown plants. However, they are prone to dropping their fruit and even dying unless extremely good care is taken to keep them well and regularly watered – this can mean three or four times a day in summer. Similarly, attention is needed to prevent the roots freezing in winter. An advantage of container culture is that the whole pot can be taken under cover to prevent frost or bird damage or to bring on earlier growth.

Use the biggest container you can manage – plastic dustbins can be converted with holes in the base and are much cheaper than pots. Fill with a good potting compost, use the most dwarfing rootstock and arrange some form of automatic watering system.

Right: It is possible to grow grape vines in containers, which is problem-free as long as you do not neglect the watering, especially in warm weather.

Below: Many herbs are suitable for containers. They can be taken indoors in the winter months to prolong the harvest season.

Good choices
- Sweet and sour cherries
- Peaches
- Apricots and nectarines
- Figs
- Grapes

Vegetables

Vegetables need the best possible conditions to give good crops: rich soil, plenty of sunlight, regular water and unchecked growing time. Remember never to crowd plants too closely together, making them compete for nutrients, light and water.

Roots and tubers

Beetroot

Easy to grow and highly nutritious, beetroot likes a deep, rich soil, so dig in well-rotted compost or manure. Sow in pots or cells under cover in early spring. Plant out or sow seeds in the open in mid-spring to early summer, 2.5cm (1in) deep and 20cm (8in) apart each way. Plants also grow well sown one seed capsule to a pot or cell and left unthinned when planting out to give little beets for pickling. Sown direct and thinned, they can be grown larger for winter storage. Avoid damaging the roots when weeding because they will bleed. Beetroot is trouble-free, but birds eat the leaves, so protect plants with netting or black cotton.

• The yellow cultivar 'Burpee's Golden' can be recommended.

• 'Boltardy' is a round red cultivar suitable for early sowing.

• The barrel-shaped types of beetroot are good for slicing and storage.

• For pickling, try to find 'Crosby's Egyptian'.

Carrots

Carrots need a light, stone-free soil to do well; lighten heavy clay soil with organic material and sharp sand. When you are digging in compost, make sure it is well rotted and friable to prevent roots from forking.

Above: The conventional red beetroot on the right and the yellow 'Burpee's Golden' on the left.

Above: It is worth trying many different carrot varieties. This one is called 'Amsterdam Forcing'.

Sow at three-week intervals, about 4cm (1³/₄in) deep, from early spring to midsummer. Station sowing every 15cm (6in) is best if you want large carrots to store, but for baby carrots broadcast sow. Rake the soil then water it thoroughly; let the water drain away. Mix the seed with sand and sow this, side to side and backwards and forwards. Cover the seed with 1cm (¹/₂in) of used sterile potting compost mixed with sharp sand. Carrots can be sown and intercropped with spring onions and leeks, all sown together.

The main problem is carrot flies, and carrots must be grown under an old net curtain, fleece or fine netting to prevent damage. Peg down the netting immediately after sowing.

There are many worthwhile cultivars.
• 'Amsterdam Forcing' is a good, quick carrot.
• 'Nantes 2' can be sown from late winter under cover right through to late summer for little ones in winter.
• 'Mokum' is a good summer carrot.
• 'Autumn King' is reliable, but a bit coarse, for winter storage.
• Roundish ones like 'Parmex' are good for shallow soils and containers.

Jerusalem artichokes

These plants, which get to 1.8–2.5m (6–8ft) tall, can be useful as quick, easy-to-grow windbreaks. However, they are difficult to eradicate, so are best confined to wild corners of the garden. Do not plant them where they are likely to overshadow other crops, and do not plant them unless you are sure you like them.

They will grow in poor soil, but for best results dig a trench, working in well-rotted manure or compost. Plant tubers 15cm (6in) deep and 60cm

(2ft) apart in each direction. Water in dry weather. Jerusalem artichokes generally seem to be immune to virtually all pests and diseases.
• Try 'Fuseau', a smooth-skinned cultivar, which is easy to prepare.

Kohl rabi

Although rarely grown, this is easy and highly nutritious. It is rather like a turnip, and can be eaten cooked or, better, raw. It will grow in relatively poor conditions, although it prefers a rich, well-drained soil and can be transplanted from a seed bed, cells or pots. Sow 2.5cm (1in) deep and plant out, 25cm (10in) apart each way, from mid-spring to late summer. Water well in dry weather and mulch to conserve moisture.

Kohl rabi is usually trouble-free, although plants will become hard and woody if they are checked while growing. Make sure they always have sufficient water and food.
• The cultivar 'Purple Vienna' is widely available, but 'Superschmelz' is better, remaining crisp and tender while growing very large.

Above: Kohl rabi is useful as a quick-growing, trouble-free catch crop.

Parsnips and Hamburg parsley

These roots take up the ground for a long time, and they cannot be recommended for gardens with limited space. They like well-drained soil but not one that has been recently manured. Avoid stony soil. Parsnips require station sowing: sow three seeds 2.5cm (1in) deep and 10cm (4in) apart each way for small types and 25cm (10in) apart for larger types. Sow from late winter to early spring, but not in cold, wet conditions. It is often better to wait and make a later sowing in mid-spring when the soil is warmer. Parsnip seed is slow to germinate and it does not keep, so use fresh each year. Thin to one seedling when they emerge and forget about them until the leaves die down, when they can be harvested.

Hamburg parsley produces a parsnip-like root. It tastes of parsley but is grown and used like parsnips. The leaves can be used like parsley.

Canker can be a problem with some cultivars. Avoid hoeing too close to the roots because damage to the shoulder can encourage canker. Carrot flies may be troublesome (see page 39). Water parsnips and Hamburg parsley regularly in dry weather to stop the roots from splitting.
• 'Avonresister' is good but small.
• 'Tender and True' is the best large parsnip.

Potatoes

Although they are easy to grow, potatoes need some care to give worthwhile yields. The soil must be enriched with organic material, and they can involve a lot of work.

Because they are susceptible to diseases spread on seed potato tubers, it's best to buy new certified stock every year. However, it's possible to grow self-saved tubers for a couple of years and then to buy new stock before yields drop or after a year troubled with disease. Save only tubers from healthy, typical plants; never save from plants that yield badly or look poor; egg-sized tubers are best; green bits do not matter.

As soon as you can each year, chit the seed by laying the tubers rose-end up in a tray, keeping them in a slightly warm, well-lit place to grow short green shoots. As soon as weeds begin to grow, plant out the seeds. Earlies need to be 10–15cm (4–6in) deep and 30–45cm (12–18in) apart each way, rose-end up; maincrops need the same depth but 60cm (2ft) apart each way. To produce many small, new potatoes, leave all the shoots on; for fewer, bigger tubers remove all shoots but one. To increase yields significantly water heavily when the flowers appear and remove the poisonous seedheads that follow.

Conventionally, the seed potato is planted in a trench. I prefer to make large, saucepan-shaped holes at the required distance, using a trowel. Add comfrey leaves to the hole, followed by sieved garden compost. Plant the seed potatoes and add some grass clippings as protection against scab. Replace the soil in the hole and firm down. Once the potatoes emerge, drag soil up around each plant to molehill size. A mulch of straw, leaves or grass clippings keeps the soil moist and protects young tubers from the sun, which would turn them green. For maincrops apply a collar of newspaper under the mulch so that even if the birds scratch away the grass or straw the tubers remain out of the light.

Organic gardeners are advised to grow early potatoes. These give lower yields but crop quickly and can be harvested before potato blight can become a problem; it usually comes after midsummer during warm, wet weather. Second earlies miss most blight attacks. The more productive maincrops need to grow on into early autumn to give full yields. Scabby patches can be avoided by mixing grass cuttings with the soil and compost. Potatoes are also affected by wireworms, eelworms and blackleg (see pages 42–3 and 45).

There are hundreds of potatoes but only a few are widely available.

- 'Sutton's Foremost', 'Epicure', 'Sharpe's Express' and 'Pink Duke of York' are good earlies.
- 'Wilja' and 'Charlotte' are good second earlies.
- 'King Edward', although low-yielding, is a good maincrop.
- 'Pink Fir Apple' is good for salads.
- 'Romano' is good for baking and chipping.

Radishes

Sow radishes anywhere you like, a few seeds at a time, every week from spring to autumn. Water in dry weather. They will tolerate most soils and are quick-growing, although they must be eaten when young and tender. Black Spanish and Japanese radishes are sown after midsummer and are more like turnips (and treated as such). Flea beetles can be a problem (see page 40).

- Try 'Cherry Belle' and 'Long White Icicle'.

Salsify and scorzonera

Like parsnips, these prefer deep, rich soil. Grow them like parsnips, sowing three seeds to a station in mid- to late spring, 2.5cm (1in) deep and 15cm (6in) apart each way. Thin to one seedling. Weed by hand because the roots are easily damaged. Water regularly, especially in dry weather, and mulch to conserve moisture. To produce young shoots in spring, cut off the leaves in autumn and earth up to a depth of 15cm (6in). These are generally trouble-free as long as they are watered regularly.

- Try 'Mammoth' for salsify and 'Maxima' varieties for scorzonera.

Swedes and turnips

Both these need a well-drained soil that is rich in humus to retain moisture. Turnips can be started in cells if they are planted out while still small, but they do best if sown direct from early spring to late summer, 2.5cm (1in) deep and 15cm (6in) apart each way. Keep well watered and mulch to conserve moisture. They will be tough and stringy if grown in dry conditions. Sow in mid- to late spring, either direct or in cells, and transplant while small to 30cm (12in) apart each way. Water well, especially in dry weather, or they will be woody. Mulch around the plants to conserve moisture.

- The best all-round turnip is 'Golden Ball', which stores reasonably well in a cool place.
- 'Snowball' is quick to grow and succulent.
- 'Acme Purple Top' and 'Marian' are recommended swedes.

Below: Turnips become tough in dry conditions, so mulch the soil to retain moisture.

Onion family

Garlic and shallots

As long as you have a sunny site and have dug in plenty of well-rotted manure or compost, these are easy to grow. Both can be grown in any spare patch in the ornamental garden, where they will discourage pests and diseases in other plants.

Garlic can be planted from mid-autumn to late winter; the earlier the better. Plant individual cloves, pointed end up, 2.5cm (1in) deep and 15cm (6in) apart each way. Shallots need shallow holes. Plant 1cm (½in) deep and 23cm (9in) apart each way from midwinter to early spring. Keep the plants weeded at all times, working by hand if necessary.

Both may be pulled out of their holes by birds or worms and will need replanting, but they are otherwise trouble-free.

• The garlic 'Long Keeper' is a good variety for cooler climates.

Above: Garlic should be harvested in the summer when the leaves begin to yellow. Loosen bulbs with a fork and leave to dry and ripen in the sun.

Leeks

These hardy plants take up little space and will do well in a rich, moist soil, although they will not do as well in hot, dry conditions. Dig in plenty of well-rotted compost or manure before planting. Sow 2.5cm (1in) deep under cover in early spring. Plant out in late spring, 15cm (6in) apart each way, and when transplanting use a dibber to make holes at least 15cm (6in) deep. Insert the leek, and water in well with dilute seaweed solution. Do not fill in the holes with earth. Hoe to keep down weeds and water regularly in dry weather. Mulch to conserve moisture.

Leeks are relatively trouble-free. 'Alvito' and 'Conora' are partly rust-resistant (see page 48).

• For autumn leeks try 'The Lyon' or 'Argenta'.
• For winter use grow 'Musselburgh'.
• 'Alaska' will stand and grow larger until late spring; it has blue foliage and can be grown in ornamental areas.

Onions

Onions like a richly organic soil, so in winter be sure to dig plenty of well-rotted manure or compost into the soil. They also prefer a sunny site. Keep young onions weeded, and water regularly in dry weather.

Onion sets are easy but are more expensive than seed. However, they give good results and avoid the problems associated with seed-grown plants. Sets are planted from late winter to mid-spring, but the earlier the better if the ground is ready. Rake to a fine tilth, then plant in shallow holes, 20cm (8in) apart each way, and keep putting them back when the birds and worms pull them up. Sets are convenient for intercropping where space is available, especially between brassicas and in ornamental areas of the garden, where they discourage pests and diseases.

Onion seed can be sown direct, but it is better to sow under cover in mid- to late winter in pots or cells. Don't worry about getting more than one plant per cell because two or three grown together will give smaller, harder onions that keep well. Harden off for a few days in a coldframe before planting. Plant out in early to mid-spring, close planting at 10cm (4in) apart each way for small, long-keeping onions and spacing to 18cm (7in) apart each way for larger ones for earlier use.

In late summer direct sow Japanese onions for overwintering. Rake the soil to a fine tilth and sow 1cm ($\frac{1}{2}$in) deep. Thin to 10cm (4in) apart each way. They will be ready before midsummer (when onions are expensive) but do not try to keep them after summer because they go off easily.

Pickling onions are sown thickly so that they crowd each other. 'Paris Silverskin' is the usual cultivar to choose, although pickling shallots are a good alternative to try.

Spring onions should be sown 1cm ($\frac{1}{2}$in) deep and 1cm ($\frac{1}{2}$in) apart in early autumn for spring use, and again in late winter and early spring for successional crops. The spring sowings can be grown with carrots as an intercrop.

If onion flies are a problem in your area grow sets, which rarely suffer from the pest, or grow under netting or fleece. If the leaves get a grey mould, dust them with wood ash, which will check the attack. If white rot or stem eelworms appear dig up and burn the affected plants (see page 42). Weed around onions by hand so that you do not damage or break the leaves or bulbs when you are cultivating soil close by.

There are many different onions available.

- 'Sturon' and 'Turbo' are excellent sets.
- 'Giant Zittau', 'Bedfordshire Champion' and 'Southport Red Globe' can be grown from seed.
- 'Senshyu Yellow' and 'Imai' are the best Japanese onions for overwintering.

Brassicas

Brassicas can be started in small pots, but the most reliable crops are sown direct in a seedbed. When seedlings are about 8cm (3in) high, lift them to break the taproot and replant in a seedbed, 8cm (3in) apart. When they are about 15cm (6in) high, transplant the seedlings. Make a deep hole at the recommended spacing for individual types. Add diluted seaweed solution and sieved compost, seaweed meal and calcified seaweed. Plant seedlings to the depth of the lowest leaves and firm well.

All brassicas suffer from bird damage, so use black cotton. To prevent cabbage root fly attacks when they are transplanted, use 15cm (6in) square pieces of old carpet, underlay or roofing felt with a slit cut in one side. Push it around the stem of the seedling and lay it flat on the ground, to prevent the flies laying eggs in the soil.

Seedlings can also suffer from root flies in pots and seedbeds. Caterpillars can be handpicked or sprayed with *Bacillus thuringiensis*, whiteflies can be controlled with soft soap if they start to increase, as can aphids. Keep the area wet to discourage flea beetles (see pages 38–43).

The worst problem suffered by brassicas is clubroot, which, once it gets into the soil is ineradicable. The best 'cure' is prevention, so never buy in brassica plants. If you must, only buy ones grown in sterile compost, not soil.

Wallflowers and stocks can carry the disease, and it may also be introduced with animal manure, which must always be thoroughly composted before use. Its virulence can be modified by heavily liming the plot before planting, and crops can be grown in pots, then transplanted to holes filled with sterile compost, so that infected soil does not touch your roots. Strict rotation of crops is essential where brassicas are concerned to prevent a build-up of the disease. Some new varieties are partly resistant.

Brussels sprouts

These can be available from mid-autumn to early spring if several cultivars are grown. Sow successively from early to mid-spring and transplant to 60cm (2ft) apart each way by midsummer in well-firmed soil. Plant them extra deep.

- 'Bedford Fillbasket' and 'Peer Gynt' are early.
- 'Icarus' gives a good late crop.
- 'Seven Hills' is recommended.
- 'Noisette' produces tiny, nutty sprouts.
- 'Rubine' has small, red sprouts.

Cabbages

For early summer cabbages start in pots under glass from midwinter on, harden off in a cold frame and plant out, 45cm (18in) apart each way, in early to mid-spring. To follow on, sow from late winter to early spring in the seedbed, planting out to 45cm (18in) apart each way in late spring. For early autumn cabbages, sow in the seedbed in mid- to late spring and plant out, 45cm (18in) apart each way, in early summer. For late autumn and early winter cabbages, sow in the seedbed in late spring to early summer and plant out, 60cm (2ft) apart each way, in midsummer. For spring cabbage, sow in mid- to late summer in the seedbed and plant out, 30cm (12in) apart each way, in early to mid-autumn.

- For early summer, plant 'Greyhound', 'Primo' or 'Hispi', followed by 'Primo', or 'Grand Prize'.
- For early autumn try 'Minicole', 'Winningstadt' and 'Red Drumhead'.
- For late autumn and into winter sow 'Holland White', 'Celtic', 'Christmas Drumhead' and the crinkly leaved 'Savoy Ormskirk'.
- For spring sow 'Offenham' and 'Spring Hero'.

Calabrese

This autumn broccoli is not hardy, and to do well it needs to be sown direct from mid- to late spring. With care, it can be started off in 8cm (3in) pots if planted out 45cm (18in) apart each way well before the root system fills the compost. It needs especially rich, moist soil. Mulch well with compost and water well in dry weather.

- 'Trixie', a new cultivar, is resistant to clubroot.
- 'Romanesco' has good texture and flavour but is more difficult to grow.

Below: A variety of calabrese called 'Mercedes'.

Above: The mini-cauliflower 'Garant' that grows particularly well on sandy soil.

Cauliflowers

Successive sowing of different cultivars will give cauliflowers almost all year round, but they are more difficult to grow than cabbages. They need very rich, moist soil, and their growth must not be checked at any stage or button-sized heads will result. Check that the level of lime is adequate, and keep the soil moist and well watered, especially in dry weather. Do not expect good results on light soils. When the curd starts to swell, bend the side leaves over to keep the light from yellowing it.

For summer and autumn cauliflowers, sow in a seedbed in early to late spring and plant out, 60cm (2ft) apart each way, from late spring to midsummer. For spring use, sow in mid- to late spring and plant out, 60cm (2ft) apart each way, in early summer. On light soils and in small gardens use 'mini-caulis', which are close planted, 15cm (6in) apart, and are best sown direct. They produce small heads, suitable for individual meals.
• For summer and autumn cauliflowers sow 'All the Year Round', 'Mexico' and 'Snowcap'.
• For spring use sow 'Armado' and 'May Star'.
• 'Purple Cape' is red and reliable.
• The most reliable mini-cauli is 'Garant'.

Chinese cabbage

Although this is grown alongside other brassicas, well-rotted manure or compost must be dug in beforehand. Sow direct, 1cm (½in) deep and 30cm (12in) apart, in rich, moist soil, or it will bolt, as will plants sown before midsummer. Sow successively from midsummer to early autumn, protecting later sowings with a cloche. Keep moist and well watered.
• 'Green Towers' is a bolt-resistant cultivar, which may do well from late spring.

Kale

This is the hardiest brassica of all and will provide greens in spring when all else fails. It is also nutritious, fairly resistant to clubroot and cabbage root flies and is not usually eaten by birds. Sow in mid- to late spring, planting out 45cm (18in) apart each way, in early summer.
• Grow 'Dark Green Curled' or 'Pentland Brig'.

Below: Curly kale, seen here among the asparagus fern, is hardy and reliable.

Sprouting broccoli

This overwintering crop is available in spring, when little else is growing. Sow in mid- to late spring in a seedbed and transplant, 75cm (30in) apart each way, by midsummer.

• Try 'Early Purple', 'Late Purple' and 'White Sprouting' for succession.

Above: Purple sprouting broccoli, one of the most reliable, nutritious and hardy of spring crops.

Leaves

Lettuces, endives and chicory

Lettuces are one of the easiest crops to grow well and yet they are often badly grown. Never sow a lot of seed at once. They can be sown in situ, 1cm (½in) deep and 15–25cm (6–10in) apart, or grown in a seedbed and planted out. Without doubt, the best way is to use multi-celled packs. Sow a few cells each of several types every few weeks through most of the year. Thin to one plant per cell and plant out as intercrops. The biggest problem is slow growth, which makes them bitter, so water thoroughly.

Salad bowl and cutting varieties are not uprooted but eaten on a cut-and-come-again basis, so make the best use of the ground. Cos lettuces are tall and need tying up to blanch them or they may be bitter. Overwintered lettuces need to be grown under cover, not so much for the warmth as for protection from the weather and hungry creatures. The popular radicchio, which is dark red, is sown 1cm (½in) deep or started in cells like lettuce and planted out 25cm (10in) apart each way from late spring to midsummer. Endives are grown like lettuces, but they must be blanched or they are too bitter. They can be cropped on the cut-and-come-again basis, so are economical on the ground. Sow from late spring to late summer, 1cm (½in) deep and 30cm (12in) apart each way. Better still, start them off in cells like lettuces.

Chicory produces heads that are grown like lettuces; they may be solid like a Cos or round and looser. They can be left until late autumn, when the roots are lifted and the foliage cut off and stored in a cool place. Then, when wanted, they are packed in sand in a warm, dark place where they start to produce solid shoots, called chicons, which are a superb addition to winter salads. If they are not lifted, chicory plants may overwinter and produce early leaves for cutting before they start to bolt.

Keep birds off the lettuce plants with black cotton and be sure to control slugs. There is a wide range of lettuces, so try many different ones

to see which you like best and grows well for you.
- 'Tom Thumb' is quick from early sowings.
- 'All the Year Round', 'Great Lakes', 'May King', 'Salad Bowl' (red and green) and 'Webb's Wonder' are good for summer use.
- 'Little Gem' and 'Lobjoits Green Cos' are good Cos lettuces.
- For overwintering try 'Kwiek' and 'Kellys' (under cover).
- Grow 'Rossa de Verona' raddichio for all purposes.
- For forcing, grow 'Brussels Witloef'.

Spinach

Leaf beet, called perpetual spinach, is easier to grow and more nutritious than real spinach, but if you want the real thing sow at intervals from early spring to late summer. Sow thinly, 2.5cm (1in) deep, and thin to 18cm (7in) apart each way. It can also be started in cells or pots if planted out while still very small. It is worth feeding the soil beforehand with a handful of seaweed meal per square metre or a bucketful of sieved compost, because it needs rich conditions, or it will bolt. Water well to encourage growth and prevent bolting. It is one of the best crops to grow through a plastic mulch because the mulch keeps the leaves away from the soil and aids growth.

For winter and early spring, prickly seeded spinach can be grown. Sow in the same way in late summer. Cloches will protect the plants but may encourage mildew.

New Zealand spinach is another non-spinach that is used and grown in the same way. It survives much better in hot, dry conditions and is more reluctant to bolt. It does need more space, and is better started in pots and planted out,

60cm (2ft) apart each way. Water well. Never allow plants to dry out or they will bolt.

Protect spinach plants from birds with black cotton and be sure to use slug traps.
- The best summer or round-seeded spinach cultivars are 'Monstrous Viroflay', 'Avanti' and 'Medania'.
- For winter try 'Sigmaleaf', which is really a summer spinach, and 'Broad Leaf Prickly'.
- 'Bergola' can be sown under cover from autumn to spring.

Swiss chard (seakale beet)

Chards are beetroot grown for their leaf stems instead of their roots, and they are treated in the same way. This is one of the most productive crops for small gardens and will carry on producing until hard winter frosts.

Sow 30cm (12in) apart each way in mid-spring and make a second sowing in midsummer for winter use. Water well in dry weather.

Slugs are the only serious problem, but ruby chard may also suffer from blackflies.
- Ruby chard is brightly coloured and is attractive in the ornamental garden.

Pods and seeds

Broad beans

These nutritious beans are easy to grow. Extra early crops of long-pod cultivars may be raised from sowings made in late autumn in mild conditions. They do best on fertile, well-drained soil. Avoid cold, wet conditions for overwintering or seeds may rot. Sow 5–8cm (2–3in) deep from late winter to mid-spring, 15cm (6in) apart each way. Provide support as they develop.

Broad beans can be affected by blackflies (see page 39), bean weevils (see page 43) and chocolate spot. Pinch out the growing and flowering tips once they start flowering to prevent blackfly attacks, or use soft soap later. Broad beans intercop well with potatoes, and summer savory helps to discourage blackflies.

- 'Aquadulce Claudia' and 'Express' are early.
- 'The Sutton' is good for small gardens.

French beans

Sow under cloches in mid-spring and in the open garden from late spring to midsummer. Sow 5cm (2in) deep and 30cm (12in) apart each way. French beans are susceptible to late frosts, cold winds and slug and bird damage, and will benefit immensely from plastic bottle cloches. Mulch after sowing with grass clippings to preserve moisture. Water in dry weather.

Below: The climbing French bean 'Blue Lake' is especially convenient for small vegetable plots.

Aphids and slugs can be troublesome.
- Highly recommended cultivars include 'Canadian Wonder', 'Radar' and 'Masai'.
- For drying as haricots try 'Brown Dutch' (although any cultivar will do).
- There are some climbing forms, which grow like runner beans but have the finer texture and flavour of French beans; try 'Blue Lake'.

Runner beans

This is an easy crop to grow, and cultivars with coloured flowers and purple beans look attractive in ornamental areas. They are highly productive, but have a coarser texture and flavour than French beans.

If your soil is very poor it will be worth improving conditions by digging in well-rotted compost before planting. Generally, however, these beans give a good crop without any special preparation. Seeds can be started off under cover in early spring, one seed per pot. Plant out in late spring after hardening off. Otherwise, sow in late spring, 5cm (2in) deep and 23cm (9in) apart. They need to be well mulched, watered and picked regularly to do well.

Runner beans need to be supported on poles, wires or strings, but netting is better and wire netting is best of all. All the supports can be suspended from posts, walls or fences. Try growing the shorter varieties up and over sweetcorn if this has been started earlier in pots and planted out. Pinch out the plants when they reach the tops of the supports to encourage bushy growth.

Runner beans may suffer from slugs and aphids when they are small.
- Among the available cultivars try 'Desirée', 'Kelvedon Marvel', 'Scarlet Emperor' or 'Butler'.

Okra

This is difficult to grow unless permanently heated conditions are available or unless it is grown in warm, sheltered areas with long, hot summers. Treat as aubergines (see page 104), but space 60cm (2ft) apart. Support with canes and pinch out tips when plants are 30cm (12in) high to encourage bushy growth.

Red spider mites, aphids and whiteflies can be troublesome (see pages 38–43).

Peas, mangetout, sugar snap and asparagus peas

Peas are more work than most vegetables, but they are so delicious fresh that they are worth the effort, and, as legumes, they enrich the soil for other crops. Peas are one of the few crops better grown in rows.

Grow short types; although they produce less, they do not need as much or as strong support, and they do not shade out other crops as much as taller ones. In dry conditions peas are quicker to germinate if they are soaked for an hour or so before sowing, and adding a dash of seaweed solution helps to disguise their smell from mice. As peas need support, grow them down the middle of a bed, and grow potatoes, brassicas, carrots or sweetcorn on either side. For succession, peas can be sown from late winter to midsummer. They can even be sown in late autumn for over-wintering, but these overwintered plants rarely do well. I have found that one good watering when the flowers are finishing will improve yields substantially.

Mangetout peas have edible pods, so podding is unnecessary when they are young and tender, but they are usually tall and rapidly get tough.

Sugar snap peas are similar but have thicker, sweeter, edible pods. They also tend to be tall, except for 'Sugar Rae'. Asparagus peas are more like a vetch than peas. The pods can be eaten when they are small and tender. They grow in poor conditions and have pretty flowers.

Use pea guards to keep birds from eating the seeds and young leaves; if mice are a problem put down traps. Do not worry about mildew as it rarely affects yields.

• The round-seeded cultivars are the hardiest, but they are not as sweet; 'Meteor' is probably the best cultivar.

• The wrinkled-seeded cultivars are sweeter, so for later sowing grow 'Early Onward', 'Greenshaft', 'Kelvedon Wonder' and 'Rondo'.

• Petits pois are just small, sweet, wrinkle-seeded peas; grow 'Lynx' or 'Waverex'.

Sweetcorn

This is a luxury that really needs to be cooked within about 30 minutes of being picked or it is not sweet.

Small cardboard tubes are ideal for sowing under cover in mid-spring. Sow a second crop direct, 2.5cm (1in) deep and 60cm (2ft) apart each way, in late spring. For sowing from seedlings dig each planting deep and wide. Water with diluted seaweed solution and add sieved compost and seaweed meal. Take the seedlings that were grown under cover and plant in the holes, with more sieved compost. Firm well and add a bottle cloche for protection. When the plant is about 30cm (12in) high remove the cloche. Add more sieved compost, earthing up around the plant to encourage rooting. Firm well and add a mulch of grass cuttings to reduce moisture loss.

When sowing in situ each site is dug and improved and the seed sown 10cm (4in) deep but covered with only 2.5cm (1in) of soil. Add a bottle cloche for protection. When the plant is about 30cm (12in) high remove the cloche. Add more sieved compost, earthing up around the plant to encourage rooting. Firm well and add a mulch of grass cuttings to reduce moisture loss.

Sweetcorn is best grown in a block to ensure pollination, and I find that potatoes, squashes or nasturtiums are a good intercrop, keeping the soil moist and providing the young shoots with extra shelter. Do not grow extra-sweet cultivars near ordinary ones, because they cross-pollinate and give poorer results. Water well when the cobs start to swell.

Grow several cultivars to give a succession.
• 'Kelvedon Glory', 'Northern Extra Sweet', 'Champ' and 'Butterscotch' are my favourites.

Shoots and buds

Asparagus
A real luxury, which takes three years before it becomes productive, but highly recommended if you have space. It has attractive foliage, so can be used in ornamental areas. It does best in a permanent bed on its own, as it takes a lot of space to yield any quantity. It can be grown under fruit (especially grapes) to save space.

Plant one-year-old crowns in early spring. Prepare a trench 25cm (10in) deep and work in plenty of well-rotted manure or compost. Soak the crowns in water for an hour, then plant in the trench 15cm (6in) deep and 60cm (2ft) apart.

Asparagus is rarely affected by pests and diseases so no special treatment is required.

• New hybrids are appearing that are all male and do not waste energy producing seed; otherwise, there is little to choose from between cultivars.

Celery and celeriac
These need careful tending and permanently moist, rich soil to grow well. They are not easy. If you want celery just for the flavour, grow it like parsley, let it self-sow and use the leaves.

Celery needs to be surface-sown in tiny pots or cells in a propagator, in late winter or early spring. The seed is difficult to sow individually, so thin early and pot up into 5–8cm (2–3in) pots. Harden off in a coldframe and plant in late spring. Plant out 30cm (12in) apart in trenches filled with well-rotted compost or manure. Protect with plastic bottles or cloches. Water thoroughly and make sure that the plants never dry out. Once they are about three-quarters grown, surround each one with a collar of newspaper and earth up to blanch them. Continue earthing up every three weeks as the plants grow.

Celeriac is started in the same way as celery and requires the same moist, rich soil. It is, however, more forgiving. No trenches are needed, but well-rotted manure should be dug in in winter. Plant out 30cm (12in) apart and keep well watered. It can be persuaded to produce a swollen root by most gardeners, and no blanching is needed. Strip off lower leaves as the root starts to swell.

It is essential to take precautions against slugs. Celery flies and carrot flies may also attack plants (see page 39).
• Two popular celery cultivars are 'Giant Pink' and 'Giant Red'.
• Celeriac is becoming widely available; look for the variety 'Monarch'.

Florence fennel

Grown for its bulb-like leaf bases, which have an aniseed flavour, Florence fennel is native to Mediterranean regions but it can be grown in more temperate areas provided it has a sunny site and moist, rich soil.

It is best sown in late spring to late summer, either in the open or in cells sown in the greenhouse, and planted out when small at 30cm (12in) apart each way. Keep watered at all times; do not let plants dry out or they will bolt and run to seed. Earth up the bases when they begin to swell and continue earthing up for 3–4 weeks. Slugs may be a problem.

Globe artichoke

Artichokes are attractive plants, which can be used in ornamental areas, but they do better given their own bed of rich soil. Rotate every third year or so. Purple artichokes taste better than the green ones but have small thorns on the buds.

Sow in pots in mid-spring and plant out seedlings the following summer, 1m (3ft) apart each way. They are also grown by planting suckers, with roots attached, taken from mature plants. They are easy to grow but may be lost in hard, wet winters unless protected with straw or cloches. Water well in dry weather.

Globe artichokes are rarely badly affected by pests and diseases.

Seakale

This is rarely grown, although it produces a tasty, nutritious crop and is attractive enough to be grown in ornamental areas.

Seakale needs a rich soil; dig in plenty of well-rotted manure or compost before planting. Sow in a seedbed and grow for a year, then transplant to

Above: A ready-to-pick artichoke head makes a delicious treat for midsummer.

Above: When seakale stalks appear, cut the head off at ground level. The crown will crop for many years.

a permanent position in late winter. Plant out in an open, sunny position, allowing 45cm (18in) each way, and grow on until autumn. They are easier to grow from 'thongs' or crowns (if available). Do not crop for two years after planting. To crop, put bottomless buckets over the crowns in dry weather in winter and cover to a depth of 23cm (9in) with a mixture of peat substitute or leafmould and sand.

Seakale is usually trouble-free, although slugs may be a problem.
• The cultivar 'Lily White' is still available.

Fruits

Aubergines
These are definitely a greenhouse crop and need continuous warm, moist conditions. Sow in pots in a propagator or on a sunny windowsill in early spring. Repot each month, then plant under cover in mid-spring in a heated greenhouse or late spring in an unheated greenhouse. Plant in border soil 45cm (18in) apart and support with canes. Water and liquid feed regularly. Allow 5–6 fruits a plant and pinch out tops when 30cm (12in) high.

Aubergines are susceptible to red spider mites and aphids, so need regular spraying with soft soap (see page 31) or the use of biological controls (see page 33).
• There are several cultivars; try 'Long Purple'.

Courgettes, marrows, squashes and pumpkins
These closely related plants need a very rich, well-manured soil to do well. They will flourish on the compost heap.

Sow in pots in the warm in mid-spring and plant out, 90cm (3ft) apart each way, in late spring once the last frost has gone. They can also

Left: A tender aubergine ready for picking. Fruits should be harvested before the seeds form and any surplus can be frozen, either sliced or as ratatouille.

Above: Pick courgettes regularly to encourage further fruiting – any that are left grow to be marrows.

Above: The pumpkin variety 'Golden Nugget' has an excellent flavour combined with a compact habit.

be sown direct under a cloche or plastic bottles in late spring. Most varieties of marrow produce long stems, which can be trained up fences or along wires. They can be grown under and over sweetcorn, if it is well established, or wound around sunflower stems. Keep well watered, especially in dry weather, and give a liquid feed when the fruits begin to appear. As they grow large, marrows, squashes and pumpkins should be propped up on bricks or pieces of wood to keep them off the soil and to prevent them from rotting. It is not worth saving the seed because plants cross-pollinate freely.

Watch out for slug damage, but otherwise they have few problems.

- Among the available courgettes look out for 'All Green Bush' and Ambassador'.
- 'Golden Zucchini' has yellow fruit.
- 'Long Green Trailing' is probably the best marrow, and 'Green Bush' is a compact form, more like a courgette plant.
- 'Custard White' ('Patty Pan') has round, flat fruit on compact plants.

- 'Golden Nugget' is the best and tastiest of the pumpkins, with a compact habit.
- 'Uchiki Kuri' is a similar Japanese form and has sweeter, nutty fruits.
- 'Mammoth' grows large, takes even more space and has little culinary value.

Cucumbers and gherkins

These need continuous warmth and moisture under cover, with a really rich soil for the best varieties, although there are inferior forms that will crop in coldframes or even out of doors in good seasons.

Greenhouse cucumbers need to be sown in pots in a heated propagator in late winter to early spring. They are then potted up until planted out in mid- to late spring. They must have continuous high temperatures of 21–24°C (70–75°F) and very high humidity. If the greenhouse is unheated, do not plant out until late spring. Plant in border soil or plant individually in 30cm (12in) pots. Support the plants by tying to bamboo canes or twisting them gently around strings attached to the roof. Pinch out the growing point when the plant reaches the roof and regularly trim sideshoots back to two leaves.

Any male flowers on cucumbers must be removed (there is no tiny cucumber behind them) before they open so that the females are not pollinated, or bitter fruit will result. Keep well watered and spray plants and paths with water to keep humidity high. Give a liquid feed regularly to promote growth. In very warm sites or with electric heating they can be planted in coldframes, but they are not easy to grow well.

- New varieties such as 'Aidas', 'Carmen', 'Fembaby' and 'Petita' are easy.

Ridge or outdoor cucumbers and gherkins are of lower quality and often have little prickles. They benefit from a coldframe or cloches, and are often better grown in a cold greenhouse or polytunnel. Dig in well-rotted manure or compost before sowing. Sow in pots in a propagator in mid-spring, keep warm and pot up until planted out, 60cm (2ft) apart each way, under cover in late spring. Alternatively, sow under cloches in late spring to early summer. Do not remove male flowers. They trail like marrows so can also be grown up fences or over a trellis once they are

Below: A large, succulent green pepper bears fruit in a warm greenhouse.

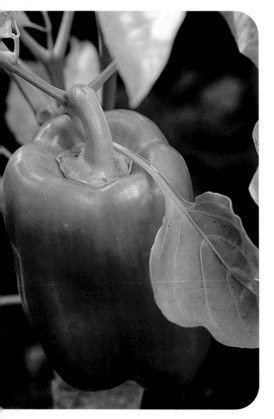

vigorous enough to fill the cloche or coldframe. Syringe regularly and mulch to conserve moisture. Give a liquid feed regularly.
• The Japanese cultivar 'Kyoto' is excellent.
• 'Marketmore' is worth trying.

They are prone to red spider mites (see page 42) and mildew (see page 47).

Sweet peppers and chilli peppers

These need warm, moist conditions, preferably in a greenhouse, although they do often succeed planted out or grown in large pots against a warm wall. Sow in pots in a propagator or on a warm windowsill in late winter to early spring. Repot monthly, then plant under cover in mid- to late spring; if it is cold plant only in a heated greenhouse. Use 30cm (12in) pots and support with canes. Pinch out the growing tip when plants are 15cm (6in) tall. Water regularly and foliar feed with dilute seaweed solution.

Chilli peppers can be very hot, despite growing in the cool, and are prolific.

They need spraying with soft soap against aphids. Keep an eye out for slug damage to ripening fruit. Interplant with basil, which likes the same conditions.
• For enormous sweet peppers grow 'Big Bertha'.
• 'Californian Wonder' and 'Canape' are also good.

Tomatoes

These need well-enriched soil. Sow in pots in a propagator in late winter and early spring for indoor crops and in mid-spring for outdoor crops. Pot up twice and keep warm until hardened off. Plant out, at 60cm (2ft) apart each way, in mid-spring under cover or in late spring to early summer outdoors.

Most cultivars are normally grown as single cordons tied to canes, with all the sideshoots rubbed off. I sometimes grow plants as double and triple cordons, because these give bigger, earlier crops. Sideshoots that are removed early on can be potted up, and they will easily root to make new plants. Indeterminate types or non-deshooted plants produce many sprawling stems, and to keep these and the fruit off the soil I place old wire baskets over the young plants, which grow up through them. These can also be covered with a plastic sheet to act as cloches while the plants establish. Outdoors they always benefit from cloches or at least wind protection with nets on stakes, and these can be used later to protect the plants from birds.

Growing under cover gives bigger yields, which come earlier. Plant the tomatoes directly into the soil in the greenhouse or tunnel rather than using pots. The extra watering and feeding can never replace a free root-run. The soil will become tired if tomatoes are grown in it year after year, so dig it out and refill with enriched, fresh topsoil every few years or so.

Feeding is not really necessary in rich, loamy soil, but it is needed by plants in poor soil or containers. Comfrey liquid (see page 16) is ideal for feeding tomatoes. For early crops be careful not to overfeed, because this produces growth instead of fruit. I find that the fruit from underfed plants tastes better, although starved ones just do badly. Do not overfeed even maincrops. Water well but not too often if plants are in the ground, without allowing them to be checked, which causes blossom end rot or splitting. In pots or containers it is harder to get an even water balance. Water tomato plants frequently and keep

Above: There is a tremendous range of tomato varieties, so grow several for different flavours. These 'Marmande' tomatoes are tasty and good for salads.

the medium constantly moist once vigorous growth starts. Tomatoes ripen best on the plant. Leave a ripe one or a banana in the greenhouse to help others to ripen.

Tomato crops rarely suffer badly from pests and diseases, especially if they are grown with French marigolds and basil. Soft soap and predators (see pages 31 and 33) will deal with whitefly infestations in the greenhouse.

Grow several different tomato cultivars for different flavours and uses.
• 'Pink Brandywine' tastes best of all but has poor disease resistance.
• 'Gardener's Delight' tastes very good.
• 'Marmande' and 'Dombito' beefsteaks produce large, tasty tomatoes, but to get really big ones limit the number of fruits to three or four to a plant at a time.
• 'San Marzano' and plum-type ones taste poor raw but are wonderful cooked.
• 'Moravi' and 'Aromata' are most reliable greenhouse varieties.

The fruit garden

Growing organic fruit is easier and makes more sense than growing vegetables. Shop-bought fruit is never really fresh, and the plants grown are chosen for their high yield, rather than for their flavour. At home you can choose old-fashioned cultivars with good flavour and high vitamin content.

Tree fruit

Apples

Apple trees are not fussy about soil or site, although very wet sites may encourage scab and canker, and they prefer a slightly acid soil. Most apples can be grown as cordons, 60cm (2ft) apart, and as espaliers, at 3m (about 10ft) apart, to give high-quality fruit and to squeeze in as many cultivars as possible in a small space. They can also be grown as fans, stepovers and festoons. Some, known as tip-bearers, such as 'Beauty of Bath' and 'George Cave', are better grown as rarely pruned dwarf bushes. If you are planning to grow apples in containers, make sure you use a semi-dwarfing rootstock.

Pollinating partners are best provided by growing several different cultivars that share a flowering period. A crab apple will pollinate most others that are also in flower.

Apples suffer infestations of several pests and diseases, such as woolly aphids, codling moths, apple sawflies, wasps, canker, scab and rot, but as long as damaged fruits are removed during successive thinnings there should still be plenty of fruit. Apply sticky bands in early autumn and check them throughout winter to catch most winter moths. Use pheromone traps to prevent codling moth maggots attacking valuable crops. Scabby patches on fruit are related to blisters and blotches on twigs and leaves, so prune these out and allow more air and light into the tree, and then mulch and feed to stimulate growth and

Below: Any apples which are not quite up to standard for eating can be made into delicious apple juice.

spray once a month with seaweed solution. This will also discourage canker 'ulcers', which often occur on poor growers. Brown, rotten patches on apples are caused by bruising or damage and then infection by spores overwintering in stems and soil. Mulching and seaweed sprays will encourage healthy growth. Small trees and bushes should be netted against birds.

- Among early croppers are 'George Cave' and 'Discovery'.
- Good late keepers include 'Ashmead's Kernel', 'Winston', 'Wagener' and 'Tydeman's Late Orange'.
- Outstanding mid-season apples include 'James Grieve', 'Orleans Reinette' and 'Charles Ross'.
- 'Bramley' is a good cooker, but 'Reverend W. Wilks' and 'Howgate Wonder' are also good.
- Some of the new cultivars are worth considering, including 'Greensleeves', 'Jonagold', 'Jupiter', 'Katja' and 'Spartan'.
- Even 'Golden Delicious' tastes good when it is grown organically at home.

Peaches, nectarines and almonds

These three plants have the same cultivation needs, and they are ideal additions to the ornamental garden. Grown as bushes, 4.5m (about 15ft) apart, peaches are easy, self-fertile and fruitful as long as they have rich, moist soil and are kept well mulched. They all do better in the sunnier drier regions, or in a greenhouse when they're best grown in containers and hand-pollinated. Nectarines will not crop as bushes and need the warmth of a sunny wall or greenhouse, but almonds can be grown as bushes or trees and do not require thinning or pruning.

Trees must be sprayed with Bordeaux mixture just before leaf-fall and again in late winter to

Above: 'Rochester' peaches are highly recommended grown as bushes, or even as specimen trees, where their beauty can be seen.

early spring to prevent peach leaf curl, which puckers and discolours the leaves and weakens the tree. The disease can be avoided if the trees are overwintered indoors or if a plastic sheet is hung over them. The sheet can be hung from the top of the wall over a fan-trained tree to keep the branches dry throughout winter and to late spring, and it will also provide protection from frost. Frosts will take off the blossoms and fruitlets in most years in temperate areas, so they must be covered on cold nights. On plants grown against walls and under cover, red spider mites can be a problem; spray frequently with water and introduce *Phytoseiulus persimilis* (predatory mite). Plants in the greenhouse can also be affected by mildew and scale insects (see pages 42 and 47).

- Among the best peaches for growing as bushes or standard trees are 'Peregrine' and 'Rochester'.

Pears

Late frosts can damage blossom, and pears are usually best grown as fans or espaliers against a sunny wall. Because they are large trees, pears are usually grown on quince rootstocks, to give small to medium trees. Pollinating partners are needed, and even partially self-fertile cultivars ('Conference', 'Docteur Jules Guyot' and 'Durondeau') give better fruits if pollinated. Pears need a fairly rich soil and suffer badly from grass competition, so clear the ground of all perennial weeds before planting.

Leaf blackening in spring is usually caused by harsh winds, but fireblight might cause the flowers and leaves to wither and brown. Prune out and burn affected shoots before the problem spreads. Leaf blistering is caused by mites; spray with soft soap. Fruits sometimes blacken and drop with pear midge maggots inside; collect these up and destroy them. Pears also suffer from winter moth, woolly aphids, codling moth, sawfly, canker, scab and brown rot, and birds and wasps can often be troublesome.

- 'Doyenné du Comice' (late autumn) is outstanding, but it needs a wall; it's pollinated by 'Beurré Hardy', 'Docteur Jules Guyot' or 'Glou Morceau'.
- Pears good as bushes include 'Beurré Hardy' (mid-autumn), 'Williams Bon Chrétien' (early autumn), 'Clapp's Favourite' (late summer) and 'Jargonelle' (late summer).
- 'Glou Morceau' is probably the best-flavoured keeper.
- 'Docteur Jules Guyot' (early autumn) and 'Conference' (mid-autumn) are ideal for a two-pear garden.
- 'Beth' (early autumn) is a compact form.
- Asian, Nashi, pears are self-fertile and trouble-free; try 'Kumoi' or 'Shinseiki'.

Plums, bullaces and damsons

Although these can be grown on dwarfing rootstock and trained, they're better grown as bushes or half-standards. They like richer

Below: Delicious purple 'Pershore' plums for jamming.

conditions than apples or pears, and near the compost heap is ideal. Both damsons and bullaces are self-fertile, but most plums need pollination partners.

Plums suffer from several pests and diseases, including rust, bacterial canker, silverleaf, plum sawflies, red spider mites and, especially, woolly aphids, although most do not affect the crops (see pages 38–49). Birds and wasps destroy most plums, and birds also take off buds in winter. Use black cotton after leaf-fall and, if possible, net to protect the fruit. Fruit moth maggots can be prevented with pheromone traps, and earwigs can be stopped by sticky bands. Gummosis may cause oozing from the bark on badly drained or acid soil. Prune only in summer to avoid silverleaf.

• It is hard to beat 'Victoria' (early autumn), even though it is susceptible to disease.
• 'Coe's Golden Drop' (early autumn) is tasty but shy to fruit.
• 'Reine Claude de Bavais' (early autumn) is a good cropper.
• 'Oullin's Gage' (late summer) and 'Marjorie's Seedling' (early autumn) are good for frosty areas.

Soft fruit

Blackberries and hybrid berries
Grow in rich, moist conditions, although they will fruit in poor soil and even in moderate shade. After planting, cut down each cane to a bud about 30cm (12in) above ground level, and because they fruit on one-year-old wood it is important to keep the old and new canes separate. Cut out old canes after fruiting.

Boysenberries (midsummer) are large and well flavoured but do not crop heavily, and the loganberry LY654 is productive and flavoursome. Tayberry has large, sweet fruits and does better in light shade than in full sun.

Despite potential problems including aphids, virus diseases, raspberry beetles, cane spot, spur blight and botrytis (see pages 38–49) these plants tend to crop heavily.

• Among the many cultivars 'Himalayan Giant' is the biggest and toughest (grow it as a boundary or trained over a fence to keep it upright); it is productive from early autumn and does not need a lot of space to do well.
• 'Bedford Giant' fruits in late summer.
• 'Oregon Cutleaf' is thornless but too late (mid-autumn) for cold areas.

Blackcurrants
These are self-fertile plants, but it is worth having several cultivars to spread the flowering and later cropping. They need rich, moist, heavy soil and must be planted deep and grown as a stool,

Below: Blackcurrants are a rich source of vitamin C.

because they fruit best on young wood. Prune in late summer by cutting out all fruited wood.

Net plants to protect from birds. Aphids can curl leaf tips in early summer; dip them in a bucket of soft soap solution. Big bud is a common problem, but in midwinter pick off the bigger, rounded buds and burn them. Reversion, a virus infection, is spread by big bud. Plants are also susceptible to mildew and leaf spot (see pages 38–49). If yields drop and do not improve with feeding, grub up the bushes and plant new ones.

• Some mildew-resistant forms are available, including 'Ben Lomond', 'Ben Sarek' and 'Ben More' (all midsummer).

• 'Mendip Cross' is a good early cropper.

• 'Westwick Choice' is late.

• 'Wellington XXX' (midsummer) is also recommended.

Gooseberries

Bushes need moisture and a rich soil, but will tolerate some shade; avoid planting in hot, dry spots. Prune after fruiting to give an erect, open-centred bush.

Mildew is a problem in dry conditions, and it spreads from the tips to the berries; keep plants well watered and mulched. Birds are the main pest, eating not only the fruit in summer but the buds in winter; leave pruning until early spring, and then wind black cotton around the bush. The gooseberry sawfly caterpillar will defoliate young bushes; put a sheet underneath the bush and shake it: the caterpillars can be picked up as they fall.

• Among the best cultivars are 'Leveller' (large green), 'Early Sulphur' (early yellow) and 'Langley Gage' (white sweet).

• If there is space for only one, grow the mildew-

Above: Gooseberries are available in widely varying flavours and can be deliciously sweet even when raw. The 'Keepsake' variety is particularly delicious.

resistant and reliable 'Invicta' variety.

• 'Rokula' and 'Greenfinch' are also both good gooseberries which are resistant to mildew.

• 'Keepsake' is a delicious variety.

Raspberries

Plant in a sheltered spot in full sun, if possible, although they will tolerate some shade. They need rich, moist soil and mulching to do really well, and add well-rotted manure or compost in the bottom of the planting trench. Mulch well in spring and water regularly in dry weather. Buy in new stock every ten years or so.

Birds are a problem, and raspberries must be netted or caged. Autumn-fruiting forms rarely suffer from maggots; but for summer fruiters rake over the mulch in winter to expose overwintering larvae to the birds. Despite raspberry beetle, cane spot, cane blight, spur blight, cane midges, wasps and various viral diseases, raspberries tend to crop heavily if new stock is bought every few years.

• 'Glen Ample', 'Glen Moy', 'Glen Magna' and 'Autumn Bliss' are good, but visit a pick-your-own outlet to try other cultivars before choosing.

Redcurrants and whitecurrants

These prefer a lighter soil than blackcurrants and will tolerate light shade. Mulch in spring and spray with liquid seaweed.

Plants must be netted to stop birds taking the fruit. They are susceptible to leaf blistering aphids, which pucker and discolour the leaves but do not affect the yields; they are cleared away with summer pruning. They may suffer from aphids, sawfly and leaf spot (see pages 38–49) but are usually trouble-free.

• There is little to choose among the different available cultivars, although 'Four Lands' is an early redcurrant.

Above: As raspberries vary in flavour go to a pick-your-own farm and try several before choosing. Try yellow raspberries which are exceptional.

Below: Redcurrants have quite a sharp flavour raw, but they reward well when cooked with other fruits and make delicious jams and jellies.

Strawberries

Plant in late summer in humus-rich, thoroughly weeded soil. For consistent cropping, replace about a third of the plants every year, because fewer and smaller fruits are borne by three-year-old plants. Buy completely new stock every five years or so.

New cultivars are more likely to be resistant to attacks of mould.

• Autumn-fruiting forms such as 'Mara des Bois' are not as sweet (they have less sun) but are still worth growing.

• 'Aromel' will fruit in autumn if the first flower trusses are removed.

• 'Honeoye' and 'Marshmello' are tasty.

• 'Royal Sovereign' is excellent but difficult to find.

Herbs

Herbs are an essential part of any garden, being both decorative and useful. Traditionally, they have been cultivated for their culinary and medicinal properties, although some have other uses, providing scents, fibres, dyes or cosmetics. They are particularly suited to the organic garden as they are virtually invulnerable to pests and diseases, and their scented flowers attract bees and other beneficial insects.

Herbs are ideal plants to grow if space is limited. With only a tiny area to cultivate it makes sense to grow small, quick-growing herbs for adding to salads and in cooking. You can even grow a few in windowboxes, pots or containers.

Many perennial herbs (see pages 116–19) are useful as companion plants, and in a large garden they can be grown in a variety of different places and picked systematically.

Perennial herbs are especially good companions for fruit trees and bushes, and as borders or hedges around other areas, especially vegetable beds. Ornamental areas can consist solely of perennial herbs, which are productive yet need little maintenance. Aromatic perennials thrive close to walls and pathways and to ornaments made of brick and stone, which retain the warmth that these plants love. Many attractive herb gardens are designed with a formal arrangement of brick or stone paths radiating from a central ornament or bird bath.

If space is limited, most perennial herbs can be grown in pots or containers, but do not expect them to flourish as vigorously as they would in the ground. Of course, in pots they can be stood under cover, in a coldframe or greenhouse, to extend their season. Do not take them into centrally heated rooms, however, as they will not do well. Container growing is ideal for mints, which are invasive and not easy to control when grown in a bed with other plants as they soon take over all the available space.

Annual herbs

Most annual herbs are best sown direct in their final position in mid-spring. They resent transplanting and will not make as much growth if started in small pots or cells. Mark out and station sow as for vegetables; most annual herbs do not need sowing or thinning to one plant per site. Alternatively, sow in small pots, pot up if necessary, then harden off and plant out after the last frost.

Basil (*Ocimum basilicum*)
One of the best-flavoured herbs, basil grows between 15 and 60cm (6–24in) tall. There are purple-leaved, tiny-leaved and lemon-flavoured

Above: Borage is grown for its pretty blue flowers.

Above: Coriander is a valuable cooking ingredient.

forms as well as the usual sweet basil. Start off in pots in the warm and plant out 20cm (8in) apart each way when all danger of frost is passed. Basil likes a warm, sheltered position, so grow alongside tomatoes or peppers, which like similar conditions. Watch out for aphids and cut the plants back before flowering.

Borage (*Borago officinalis*)

Borage, which gets to 60–90cm (2–3ft), tends to sprawl so is best at the back of borders. Sow in position, thin to 45cm (18in) apart and allow to self-seed thereafter. With occasional trimming, the plants can be in flower most of late spring and summer. The blue flowers are attractive to bees.

Caraway (*Carum carvi*)

Grow caraway, which will get to 60cm (2ft), in a sunny site and rich soil. Sow in position and thin to 20cm (8in) apart in spring or autumn. If left to flower in the second year it may self-seed.

Chervil (*Anthriscus cerefolium*)

This herb, growing to 30cm (12in), is like parsley but is easier to grow and has a milder flavour.

Sow from early spring to late summer in partial shade in a light, well-drained soil and thin to 15cm (6in) apart. Chervil will self-seed if left to flower, and if plants are cut down before flowering they will produce new crops of fresh foliage.

Clary sage (*Salvia sclarea*)

This handsome and stately herb, which grows to 60–90cm (2–3ft) in height, is a member of the sage family; its lilac flowers are showy and are attractive to bees. Sow the seeds in pots and plant out 30cm (12in) apart. Pick the leaves before flowers appear.

Coriander (*Coriandrum sativum*)

Plants grow to 30–60cm (1–2ft) tall. Sow in position about 25cm (10in) apart in late spring, choosing a site with full sun and rich soil.

Cumin (*Cuminum cyminum*)

A short plant, 15–30cm (6–12in) tall, cumin needs a warm, sheltered site and a well-drained soil. Station sow in early summer at 5cm (2in) apart. Support the plants with sticks to stop seedheads falling over and getting dirty.

Above: Curled parsley is milder than flat-leaved.

Above: Pick summer savoury as its flower buds form.

Dill (*Anethum graveolens*)
Dill plants grow to 90cm (3ft) tall. Sow seeds direct or in pots and plant them out 30cm (12in) apart in full sun and a rich soil. If they are left to flower, dill attracts hoverflies.

Marigold (*Calendula officinalis*)
Pot marigolds grow to 60cm (2ft). Sow in pots or direct in position 30cm (12in) apart from early spring to early autumn, and allow to self-seed. This is also a useful companion plant (see pages 66–9).

Parsley (*Petroselinum crispum*)
Parsley grows to about 30cm (12in). The bigger, continental, plain-leaved variety (*P. crispum* 'Italian') has more flavour than the common curly-leaved form.

Parsley is biennial, so flowers in the second year after sowing; leave to seed because self-sown plants are always best. Sow soaked seed on the soil surface and barely cover the seed. The seeds can take a long time to germinate. Sow once in spring and again in autumn for two years running, then use the self-sown seedlings that

appear. Thin plants to 15cm (6in) apart. Parsley revels in rich moist conditions and can stand moderate shade.

Rocket (*Eruca vesicaria* subsp. *sativa*)
Rocket, which gets to 60cm (2ft), is easy to grow but tastes best when grown quickly in moist conditions. Sow in pots or stations 15cm (6in) apart from early spring to early autumn. It is susceptible to flea beetles.

Summer savory (*Satureja hortensis*)
Plants grow to 45cm (18in). Sow shallowly in pots or direct at 15cm (6in) apart. It can be dug up and potted to put under cover for winter use.

Perennial herbs

Most perennial herbs will tolerate, and indeed often prefer, drier, poorer soils than annual herbs. Many are native to the Mediterranean region and need sunshine and a light well-drained soil to do well. It is the combination of damp and cold that kills them, and they may need some shelter or a cloche to come through bad winters – growing them against a wall is often sufficient help. In well-sheltered or town gardens most perennial herbs will last for many years. Almost all are good at suppressing weeds, suffer from few pests and diseases and need little maintenance apart from cutting back dead, overgrown and excessive growth.

Most are best bought as young plants rather than grown from seed. Many are easily grown from cuttings or dividing existing plants, so visit your friends' gardens with something to trade. Do not divide or move herbs in autumn or winter, and plant up a new herb bed in spring. Cutting back most herbs each spring removes withered growths and produces a flush of new shoots. Leave pruning until spring so that the old growth protects the new against bad weather. Take care not to cut back too far, or the plant may die; go no further than where live green shoots emerge from the older wood.

Bay (*Laurus nobilis*)

Bay trees can be anything from 90cm to 5.5m (3–18ft). Small shrubs are rather tender, especially suffering from harsh winds, and are easily killed by frost. Grow in a warm, sheltered position, or in tubs, which can be taken under cover in winter (although they are then more prone to pests). Once established, bay becomes a tough, medium-sized tree. It can be attractive as a specimen if trimmed into shape. Bay is difficult to propagate.

Bergamot (*Monarda didyma*)

A herbaceous plant, to 90cm (3ft), with beautiful scarlet flowers, bergamot is well suited to ornamental areas, liking rich, moist soil and partial shade. Divide the clump to propagate and replant every third year.

Chives (*Allium schoenoprasum*)

Chives, which grow to 30cm (12in) in height, can be started from seed or separated from existing clumps, which anyhow will benefit from being divided every other year. Plant them as neat and effective border edgings and remove the flowering heads from alternate plants to get both flowers and foliage. Grow under fruit trees and roses for their companion effects: the flowers attract beneficial insects, especially bees.

Fennel (*Foeniculum vulgare*)

An upright, stately plant, to 1.5m (5ft), fennel can be grown in ornamental areas – the bronze form (*F. v.* 'Purpureum') is particularly attractive. It likes an open, sunny position. Propagate the green form from seed or both by division in spring. Replant clumps 60cm (2ft) apart. It self-seeds readily, so remove flowerheads as they fade if you don't want it coming up everywhere. The flowerheads will attract hoverflies.

Feverfew (*Tanacetum parthenium*)

This short-lived perennial, to 45cm (18in), self-seeds with a vengeance. It is a good foil for other plants, the golden form being particularly cheerful. It is an excellent companion plant, discouraging pests, making it especially worth growing as a space filler.

Horseradish (*Armoracia rusticana*)

Horseradish will grow to 60cm (2ft). It is usually started from plant cuttings and needs well-cultivated soil because the roots go deep. Plant at the bottom of the garden or in an out-of-the-way spot, as it spreads by the roots and is hard to eradicate once established.

Above: Lavender is both decorative and fragrant.

Above: The showy leaves of variegated lemon balm.

Lavender (*Lavandula* spp.)

The gorgeously perfumed shrub, 30–90cm (1–3ft), will attract bees and butterflies. There are many forms, in a range of sizes and flower colours. Plant in well-drained soil in a sunny position.

Lemon balm (*Melissa officinalis*)

This plant, which grows to 60cm (2ft), resembles a mint but does not have the tendency to spread. Compact and dense, it excludes weeds when planted 45cm (18in) apart and will flourish almost anywhere. There is a yellow variegated form, which is especially valuable in ornamental areas.

Lemon verbena (*Aloysia triphylla*)

The shrub, which grows to 90cm (3ft), has an exquisite lemon sherbet scent, which the dried leaves retain for many months. Easily grown from cuttings, it is not hardy and gets killed above ground by hard frosts. Plant 90cm (3ft) apart against a warm wall and protect the roots from damp and cold; they sprout like fuchsias in spring. It can be kept in a pot and overwintered under cover or as a houseplant but is then susceptible to aphids and red spider mites.

Lovage (*Levisticum officinale*)

Lovage is a herbaceous plant, to 2m (6ft), which grows best in moist, shady spots. Propagate by root division or seed. The flowerheads attract hoverflies.

Marjoram (*Origanum*)

There are several varieties, all of which are similar to oregano and grow to about 30cm (12in). All prefer a sunny position. Propagate by seed for the best-flavoured ones, which are grown as annuals except in warm climates, and by root division for the tougher perennials. These latter tend to form low mounds, which make them useful as informal edging or to go under fruit trees and bushes. There is an attractive golden form that turns a butter-cream yellow in summer and reverts to green in winter. In flower, marjorams attract bees and butterflies.

Mint (*Mentha* spp.)

There are many species and forms of mint, which grow to 45–90cm (18–36in). They are invasive. Never put mints in with other herbs as the roots penetrate everything. Grow them in pots, containers almost submerged in the soil or in beds

Above: Rosemary can be picked all year round.

Above: Red sage is a beautiful and aromatic plant.

surrounded by concrete or regularly cut grass. Cool, refreshingly scented forms, such as eau-de-cologne mint (*M.* x *piperita*) and spearmint (*M. spicata*), suit ornamental areas, as do golden and silver variegated, yellow, grey and curly forms, which are mostly less vigorous. Mints make cheap and effective, low-maintenance groundcover for large areas, especially under trees, and they encourage bees and beneficial insects.

Rosemary (*Rosmarinus officinalis*)

Rosemary, which grows to 60cm (2ft), is not hardy but usually survives in colder climates if given a warm spot against a wall and well-drained soil. It makes a good hedging plant if kept well trimmed, otherwise it tends to sprawl. It will also grow in a pot under cover. It is easily propagated from cuttings in spring. The flowers are loved by bees.

Sage (*Salvia*)

Easily grown from cuttings or seed and getting to 60cm (2ft), sage needs replacing every few years as it becomes straggly and resents pruning. The red form has a fine flavour; the more compact, multi-coloured sages are not hardy.

Sweet cicely (*Myrrhis odorata*)

Plants grow to 1m (3ft) tall. Sow in autumn in light shade and transplant 60cm (2ft) apart in spring. The plant's fern-like leaves are decorative.

Thyme (*Thymus*)

Thyme is low-growing, to 20cm (8in), so goes well under fruit trees and bushes if it is sunny enough. Thymes will thrive in poor, dry situations and can be grown from seeds or propagated from cuttings. There are many forms, with a range of scents, colours and shapes, and they can be attractive in ornamental beds. Look out for the caraway-flavoured *T. herba-barona* and for the colourful *T. pulegioides* 'Bertram Anderson' (also sometimes sold as 'Anderson's Gold'). The flowers are attractive to bees.

Winter savory (*Satureja montana*)

Summer savory tastes better but this is shrubbier, to 30cm (12in), and survives most winters. It grows easily from seed, which should be surface sown and not buried. Plant out in a sunny position and well-drained soil, 23cm (9in) apart each way. In flower it attracts bees.

The ornamental garden

Being an organic gardener means, wherever possible, not using anything anywhere that may harm life so we no more want to apply pesticides or herbicides to our lawn and roses than to our cabbages. However, when we think of the ornamental garden our attention changes from production to become more focused on the aesthetics. It's actually very easy to produce usable crops organically but to get a plant to have a perfect appearance is more difficult. To get many plants to do so over the whole year is harder still. That's why people who grow for show often use so many sprays and have to keep doing so to prevent any blemish appearing.

Fortunately we have generally selected our ornamental plants because they are mostly relatively reliable. Only a few of the most highly bred or specialized plants, such as roses, may require much actual pest and disease control. The selection of plants at your local nursery or garden centre will mainly consist of those that suffer few problems other than the usual ones of slugs, snails, birds, cats and the weather!

Below: Sweet peas, larkspur and rudbeckia can be grown among the vegetables in the raised beds to create a cottage-garden look.

Ornamental plants in the organic garden

Most importantly, the wonderful mix of plants with overlapping flowering seasons in beds and borders provides for many more beneficial insects than a vegetable bed or orchard. Furthermore the mixing of such widely diverse plants makes it hard for any pest or disease to spread widely. (The various rusts and mildews and even most aphids that appear on many garden plants at about the same time are not moving from one to the other but are different strains appearing because the conditions in general suit them.)

Lawns are generally a monocrop and so need more care, but, if treated as a rough sward with clovers, daisies, thymes and camomile all mixed in, will become much healthier, need less attention and be more interesting – especially for children.

Ecology in the ornamental garden

Balancing the physical niches and habitats we can fit into ornamental gardens, from coarse mulches, dense groundcover, beehives and water features to bird boxes and dovecotes, also enables more forms of life to prosper. Thus there is usually ample fertility and rarely do most ornamental areas need additional feeding other than mulches. Indeed they can often be robbed of leaves, grass clippings and prunings to feed the productive areas. Ideally of course the ornamental beds and borders are near the vegetable beds so the beneficial insects can also benefit the crops.

There is a fashion for growing native and imported wild plants which is fine if these are from reputable growers but we must be careful not to deplete wild stocks to fill our gardens. This especially applies to wild bulbs but many other plants, and even materials such as water-washed limestone rocks, are going the way of extinct animals.

> The wonderful mix of plants in beds and borders provides many more beneficial insects than a vegetable bed

Below: A rampant honeysuckle creates a natural arch over a path bordered by daphne and ferns, enticing any wandering explorer to creep through.

Below: Single-colour combinations like this one work well, partly because they highlight the shape and form of the blooms and leaves of each plant.

Organic lawn care

Lawns and grass paths make up much of the typical garden. The uniform green shows off plants to perfection, but these areas take a lot of work and cash to maintain.

If you have a small garden think carefully about dispensing with grass altogether: this will not only do away with the lawnmower and the need to have somewhere to store it but will also liberate ground space for more interesting plants. Areas for sitting or sunbathing could be hard-surfaced or gravelled instead and surrounded or patch-planted with low-growing plants such as camomile and thymes.

In a large garden grass is the most sensible groundcover. It is relatively easy to keep neat and tidy, even if it is rather time-consuming. Grassed areas can be established in three ways: by seeding, by turfing and by cutting the natural cover regularly.

Seed

Sowing is not expensive, but it is quite hard work. The area must be dug, weeded, levelled and raked to make a seedbed, and all stones and rubbish removed. Incorporate ground rock dusts, ground seaweed and lime or calcified seaweed to enrich the soil. The first flushes of weeds can be raked or flame-gunned to remove them. The area is then sown in spring or autumn with grass seed.

> Sow a mixture of plants such as camomile and daisies with grass

Tough-wearing recreational ryegrass mixtures are a better choice than the less competitive fine grasses, which look good but do not take hard wear. The fine grasses also prefer acid conditions, which encourage mosses and weeds.

Sow a mixture of companion plants with the grass, such as clovers, camomile, creeping thyme, daisies and yarrow. The mixtures are more interesting and ecologically sound, as well as staying greener when there is a drought. After sowing, rake in the seed, firm it down and hang up bird scarers. Give the young grass a cut and roll when it is 5cm (2in) high and keep the usage light for a growing season.

Turf

Although it is the most expensive way to grass an area, it requires less work than seeding and gives more rapid results. It can only be done well early in spring or autumn with damp conditions and/or frequent watering. The area still needs to be dug, enriched and levelled, but much less thoroughly. Stubborn perennial weeds, like dandelions, must be dug out, but annual weeds can be ignored as they will mostly be killed.

Gardeners should be aware that much turf comes from old meadowland and is frequently pretreated with inorganic fertilizers and herbicides.

Natural cover

Cutting the natural groundcover regularly is a slow method of getting a good sward, but it produces the most ecologically balanced mixture of plants with the minimum of work and expense. The process is the same as for regularly maintaining or improving an existing lawn, and consists of making the conditions suitable for grasses and unsuitable for most other plants.

If the area is initially too rough for a mower, use a strimmer or brushcutter for the first cuts. Once the growth is down to a rough sward, keep cutting once a week from early spring to late autumn, returning the clippings and slowly reducing the height of cut. This kills almost all tall weeds. Acid-loving weeds are discouraged, and tougher grasses can be aided by liming twice a year with calcified seaweed or dolomitic lime. Patches of clover, which stand out green in a drought, are blended in by sowing clover seed in the remaining areas: clovers improve the lushness of the sward.

Scarifying

In autumn or spring use a wire rake to scarify the lawn. This is hard work but benefits the lawn. Scarifying produces a mass of thatch for use as a mulch or for composting, but this needs to be moistened with liquid feed to rot down quickly. Follow scarifying by raking in a mixture of ground seaweed, rock dusts and grass seed (with sharp sand for heavy soils) and calcified seaweed. This same feed can be used each spring, but it is better to use diluted urine sprinkled over the turf. It is absorbed rapidly, giving lush growth.

Rosette weeds, such as plantains and thistles, may survive scarifying, cutting and soil improvement treatments, but they can be hand-pulled with a sharp knife, severing deep underneath to stop regrowth.

Cutting

Regular cutting is an effective weed-control measure, best done with a rotary mower that can collect the clippings. Cylinder mowers are not as good in damp conditions or with longer growths. Mowers that leave the clippings build up too much thatch.

Ideally, cut the grass once a week, but vary the height through the season to control growth. The first and last cuts should be high: 5–8cm (2–3in). Return the clippings to the surface as worms are actively eating them in spring and autumn. The spring cuts should decrease in height to 2–3cm (1–1¼in) by mid-spring, and remain there until midsummer, removing and returning the clippings alternately.

From midsummer raise the height to 3–5cm (1¼–2in) to keep the grass greener and more drought-resistant, and then to 5–8cm (2–3in) from late autumn, removing the clippings until the last leaves fall. Keep the mower blades sharp to make the job easier.

Strimming

A strimmer can do the edges and around tree trunks and get into awkward and difficult spots. It is also good for trimming grass to different heights. Either side of a mown path in a wild area or orchard, for example, the grass can be kept about 30cm (12in) high, so it does not fall over the path. Cutting grass with a strimmer can provide a good environment for bulbs, primroses, cowslips and violets, as the area can be kept neat without becoming overgrown and choking out these little treasures.

Planning an organic garden

Before you plan your garden it is important to consider what you want from it. Is it to add value to your property, give you an interest in life, impress your friends – or is it just for the exercise? Do you need to provide a play area for children? If you want to grow fruit and vegetables, which ones do you want and when? After all, if you always go on holiday in late summer there is not much point planting early apples. Similarly, do you want to grow flowers for cutting or for outdoor beauty?

Details

There should be somewhere to sit, but is it to be an outdoor room or will you enjoy a vista from a window? If you want privacy, effective screening may be more important than saving money or maximizing self-sufficiency. Once you know what the parameters are then it is much easier to plan around them. Consider and plan a garden in the same way you would buy a new car or refit the kitchen – and be similarly prepared to spend a realistic amount of money.

> Choose the areas you want for food production first

Planning on paper

It will help to make a scale plan showing the boundaries, walls, service pipes, immovable objects (such as fuel tanks), solid paths, trees, major shrubs and so on, which are difficult to alter. Given time and money anything is possible in garden design, but it is much easier to work around the more permanent features than to alter them. On the other hand, areas of grass, vegetable plots, beds and borders can be moved around or altered at will. Choose the areas you want for food production first, as these need the best sites, then add other areas as space allows.

Looking at the plan will help you to see the garden as a whole, so you can organize it more rationally. Try to get the maximum use out of each item. For example, position a shed so that it shelters a bed and so that the largest blank wall faces the sun: you can then train a fruit bush against it. Put hedgehog nests underneath the floor and bird boxes under the eaves. The overflow from the water butts can be fed to a pool.

Garden features

There are many features that can be added to a garden, in much the same way as doing a house conversion – greenhouse, pond, fruit cage, hen run and so on. You do not have to have conventional front and back gardens – you can have your garden any way you like, with vegetables in the front and flowers at the back, or even just have a single, enormous fruit cage or a woodland area full of naturalized bulbs and a pond.

Getting started: organic dos and don'ts

✓ **Do** recycle all garden and household wastes for compost and reuse.

✓ **Do** maximize the natural system of checks and balances by growing a wide variety of plants.

✓ **Do** create habitats for birds and animals, especially by supplying water in the form of ponds and pools.

✓ **Do** stop using all herbicides. Instead, use the recommended methods of weed control (see pages 50–3), which usually involve no more work and are more pleasant and safer.

✓ **Do** stop using most insecticides, which are rarely necessary, though a few of the least harmful ones can be used as a last resort (see page 31).

✓ **Do** stop using most fungicides (except those described on page 31).

✓ **Do** use companion planting to outmanoeuvre pests and avoid diseases (see pages 66–9).

✗ **Don't** use soluble fertilizers, although they can be used up if greatly diluted and watered onto grass in spring when they will be taken up rapidly with little danger of run-off.

✗ **Don't** use peat.

✗ **Don't** use unecological plants, such as imported wild bulbs and bedding plants.

✗ **Don't** use plastic products when natural or longer-lasting alternatives are available.

Left: The selection of fragrant thymes planted beneath the log seat make it an especially pleasant place to take a break.

Herbs are useful, easy to grow and attractive to beneficial insects, and every garden should have space for at least a few, especially as herbs do not need much space or attention.

Hard surfaces

One of the most essential areas in any garden is somewhere to sit and relax outside – after all, this is one of the most important aspects of gardening. Hard standing, slabs or even gravel are more practical than grass and take far less upkeep. A patio must be easily accessible from the house, ideally extending out from a conservatory or kitchen, or it will rarely be used.

Patios in sunny positions soak up heat and give early ripening crops of fruit planted around them, especially grapes, which can be wound round posts or over wires. Varieties of creeping thyme and camomile will grow happily in holes or between slabs and give an exquisite scent when walked on. The patio can be edged with scented plants and aromatic herbs to add more sweet smells and help to discourage flies and mosquitoes. Bird boxes fixed to the wall and under the eaves can give extra interest and pest control; a bird table and bird bath will attract even more birds.

Below: For most people, flowers are a very important element of garden design. They contribute beauty and charm, and provide nectar and pollen for beneficial insects. The border shows bergamot and golden feverfew in the front with a pear tree on the right and a mix of phloxes behind.

Garden size

Although most of us would prefer a larger garden, it is surprising what can be done even with a tiny one. In a small garden you can produce quantities of fruit, vegetables and flowers with the same amount of time and effort that in a larger plot would be spent just cutting the grass. Moreover, in a small area any money spent is much more effective: you can buy slow-growing evergreen shrubs or build low-maintenance features, such as paved areas, whereas in a larger garden far more investment is needed.

One advantage of a larger garden is the extra privacy, especially if you have room for an informal hedge and windbreak. An extra benefit for the organic gardener is the isolation that comes with a well-hedged garden: spray drift, pests and disease spores from other gardens are less likely to arrive on your plants. In addition, the extra space for plants and habitats means that more forms of beneficial wildlife can be encouraged and retained, aiding pest control.

> There is no reason, by-laws allowing, why even the smallest garden should not have a chicken or two

A large garden also contributes plenty of prunings, grass clippings and leaves to compost for use in the vegetable beds and elsewhere. With more land the vegetable plot can be less intensively cropped, and longer rotations and green manure leys will give better crops, less prone to disease. There is also room for livestock which can convert your waste to eggs or meat, and provide a source of high-value fertilizer – although there is no reason, by-laws allowing, why even the smallest garden should not have a chicken or two.

Small town garden

Gardens in dense urban areas often enjoy greater shelter and warmth than those in more open country. Brickwork, tiles and pavements store heat, while buildings reduce low-level wind. Heat is also produced by people, buildings and cars, and there are often higher levels of carbon dioxide. All this warmth means that the growing season begins several weeks earlier. The last frost of spring always comes much later in pretty little valleys than it does in the city nearby.

Below: Hens are worth keeping for the fertility they return to the soil – and, of course, for the eggs.

Size does not so much limit the kind of garden as the number of internal subdivisions. You cannot sensibly fit a fruit cage, a rose border, a vegetable plot, a lawn and a water feature into a

Above: A pond provides a valuable habitat for wildlife as well as being attractive in its own right.

Below: Beehives work well in a semi-wild area which is set slightly apart from the rest of the garden.

3 x 3m (10 x 10ft) plot. However, you could make a beautiful and productive combination from a couple of these features. So concentrate on one or two of the options rather than trying to squeeze in as many as you can.

Even the tiniest plot has room for herbs, in pots and containers if not a whole bed of them, and where there is space a salad bed gives valuable returns. A patio area is much better value in all weather conditions than a small piece of grass. With scented plants and a small pond, you can create a tranquil little retreat from the hurly-burly of life. Fruit can be grown trained on walls and as screens, or even in large pots or containers. There may be room for a small vegetable patch or an ornamental area with productive plants.

There is always room for a compost bin and even for bees. Beekeeping is ideal for town gardeners – bees add life and interest to the garden, are productive and thrive on the longer, milder seasons and wide range of urban plants. They are more productive the more attention they receive, so are ideal if you have a small garden and plenty of spare time. Nest boxes and food for birds and hedgehogs can also be squeezed into the tiniest plots.

Larger suburban garden

For most people the typical garden is divided up into several areas, often with a fairly formal front garden and enough space to produce significant amounts of fruit and vegetables if well planned. This is, perhaps, the optimum size for most gardeners without much spare time, as the entire area can be kept attractive and productive without extra help. The larger garden does need careful planning and good routines, because otherwise too many chores eat into the time. Provided the work is organized so that it is spread over a few hours a week rather than being left so that the garden becomes unmanageable, it is possible to keep everything under control.

There should certainly be room for a fruit cage, greenhouse, vegetable plot and fruit trees, which are best placed as far from the house as practicable. Ornamental areas with lawns, patio, a pool and the herb garden should be as near as possible to the house for convenience.

When deciding on other features, it is probably better to concentrate on a few, rather than trying to cram them all in. That way, each can have sufficient space to be worthwhile. For example, it may be preferable to have vines or an asparagus bed but not both.

Large country garden

If you have up to 4,000 square metres (1 acre), what and how you grow is mainly limited by time and money, but then the garden needs either rigorous planning and/or ruthless maintenance or hired labour. I have squeezed more and more into my country garden, but it does take up the equivalent of every weekend throughout the year to stay on top of it. This is the optimum size for a keen gardener – any larger and it needs to be simplified in many areas or you need help.

Intensive methods are better replaced with extensive ones – half-standard trees in a grassed orchard rather than trained cordons; vegetables on the flat instead of in raised beds; fewer, bigger, more shrubby borders with sweeping curves and less edging. Grass-cutting is effective for maintaining large areas neatly but is one of the most time-consuming chores, and it may be a good idea to hire labour for this rather than for the more enjoyable work.

Ease of access, good pathways and locating the least visited areas farthest away are vitally important – a lot of time can be wasted going backwards and forwards to fetch tools. The space available allows for a wide range of wildlife habitats, as well as a hen run and a small pond. A garden this size should be self-sufficient in fertility.

Very large country garden

With one hectare (2.5 acres) or more, almost any garden imaginable can be created. You could certainly become self-sufficient in fruit and vegetables, and would be able to keep whatever livestock you have time for. In order to minimize labour, large areas need to be simplified, grassed and cut or strimmed regularly, enabling you to feed the rest of the garden with clippings as mulch and fertility.

> Without careful planning, too much space could prove more of a curse than a blessing

Machinery and hired labour become a necessity for many more of the tasks, although four-legged lawnmowers can replace this to a great extent. Gardening as such becomes landscaping around the house, and a large garden becomes more of a larger suburban garden with a couple of acres of paddock or private woodland extending out from it. Without careful planning, too much space could prove more of a curse than a blessing!

Garden plans

With planning, even the tiniest garden can incorporate several organic features. The two plans here should give you some good ideas. The small plot is 10m x 8m (32ft x 26ft) and the large garden is 21m x 14m (68ft x 46ft). Both are thickly planted or mulched.

1 **Worm compost bins** are particularly ideal for small gardens and can be tucked away in shady corners.

2 **Water butts**, fed from house gutters, are connected to each other with syphons to multiply capacity. In the large garden, water butts can also be located near the greenhouse.

3 **Herb bed** needs plenty of air and light.

4 **Vegetable beds** need full light and air. They are roughly 1m (1yd) wide with concrete stepping-stone paths between them to save space. Each bed is aligned north to south to catch maximum sun.

5 **Ornamental fruit cage**, painted black and decorated with finials. This is both attractive and practical.

6 **Small greenhouse.** This is the best value use of your garden space. Whether it is a lean-to against a south-facing wall or free-standing, it will need full sun. An ideal site is next to the house so that you can make use of the house's central heating system.

Small garden, south facing

7 **Larger greenhouse** located at the end of the garden in full sun.

8 **Small pool**, with sloping rough edges, one of mud, to allow wildlife easy access to the pool. A metal safety grille should be fitted just beneath the water surface to make the pool safe for children.

9 **Large pond**, to allow you more scope for attracting wildlife.

10 **Bird boxes.** Find space for as many as possible on walls, under eaves and in every dense shrub and evergreen.

11 **Ladybird and lacewing nests.** Attract these beneficial insects with bundles of hollow stems and sticks hidden in dry nooks.

12 **Rotting logs** form part of the pool habitat for beetles and dragonflies and cover pots that have been buried to provide homes for frogs and toads.

13 **Pile of stones, tiles, plates and bottles**, well hidden under evergreen shrubs and well away from the vegetables, provides a habitat to encourage other small creatures.

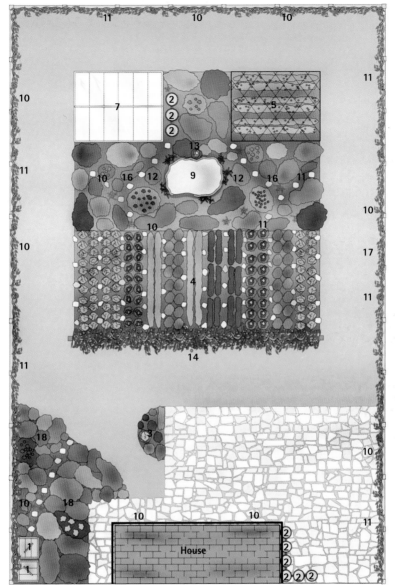

Large garden, south facing

14 **Cordon or espalier apples** create a screen and allow you to fit more varieties into a small space. These will need supports and careful pruning.

15 **Tree removed.** In a small garden any tree takes too much light and space and should go unless it is productive, protected or much loved.

16 **Lawn removed** so that all space is either productive or ornamental and there is no need for a lawnmower or for storage for one.

17 **Fence covered with climbers** to soften and disguise boundaries and optimize planting space.

18 **Thickly planted and mulched,** with small stepping stones as paths.

A year in the garden ~ Spring

	Plant	Sow	Feed	Mulch	Spray	Prune
Early spring	Artichokes, asparagus, garlic, onion sets, potatoes and shallots Evergreen shrubs and trees	Under cloches: beetroot, broad beans, cabbages, cauliflowers, carrots, chards, herbs, kohl rabi, leeks, lettuces, parsnips, peas, radishes, salsify, scorzonera, spinach, spring onions and turnips; sweet peas	Spring greens with comfrey liquid or seaweed solution	Spread everywhere	Everything with diluted seaweed solution	Evergreens and conifer hedges Hollow-stemmed and borderline hardy shrubs
Mid-spring	Onion seedlings and potato sets Perennial herbs Evergreen trees and shrubs	Under cloches: beans (broad, French, runner), brassicas (most), carrots, fennel, kohl rabi, leeks, lettuces and salad crops, parsnips, peas, radishes, salsify, scorzonera, spinach, swedes and turnips; herbs; sweet peas		Spread everywhere	Everything with diluted seaweed solution	Early-flowering shrubs as flowers fade Remove seedheads from bulbs as they die back
Late spring	Courgettes and marrows, ridge cucumbers and sweetcorn	Under cloches: courgettes and marrows, gherkins, melons, pumpkins, ridge cucumbers, sweetcorn and tomatoes; half-hardy flowers In the open: beans (broad, French, runner), brassicas (most), carrots, fennel, kohl rabi, leeks, lettuces and salad crops, parsnips, peas, salsify, scorzonera, radishes, spinach, swedes and turnips; herbs; sweet peas and wallflowers	Tomatoes and pot plants with comfrey liquid or seaweed solution Incorporate compost with all transplants	Spread under and around potatoes	Everything with diluted seaweed solution	Early-flowering shrubs as flowers fade

Spring

	Fruit	Routine tasks	In the greenhouse	Lawns and grass	Containers	General	
Early spring	Remove old canes of autumn-fruiting raspberries Spray peaches and almonds with Bordeaux mixture Plant grape vines, soft fruit and rhubarb	Compost, dig in or invert green manures	Sow aubergines, cucumbers, peppers and tomatoes	Feed with sieved compost or seaweed solution Cut weekly once in growth, leaving clippings Move, lay and repair turf		Protect early flowers and buds against frost Replace sticky bands if necessary	
Mid-spring		Weed regularly	Sow courgettes and marrows, gherkins, melons, pumpkins, ridge cucumbers, sweetcorn and tomatoes Sow half-hardy flowers	Cut weekly Use clippings for mulch	Top dress permanent plantings	Put down slug pubs Look for signs of pests and diseases Check sticky bands Protect tender flowers, fruitlets and plantlets against frost	
Late spring	Remove badly placed and overcrowded branches on apricots and peaches	Weed regularly Water autumn and spring plantings		Cut weekly Use clippings for mulch		Tie in and support climbers and tall herbaceous plants Put down slug pubs Check sticky bands Look for signs of pests (especially aphids, cabbage white caterpillars and red spider mites) and diseases Protect flowers, fruitlets and plants against late frosts	

A year in the garden ~ Summer

	Plant	Sow	Feed	Mulch	Spray	Prune
Early summer	Transplant brassicas and leeks	Beetroot, chicory, endive, kohl rabi, lettuces and salad crops, spinach, swedes and turnips; biennial and perennial flowers	Tomatoes and pot plants with comfrey liquid or seaweed solution .... Incorporate compost with all transplants	Spread under and around potatoes	Everything with diluted seaweed solution	Deadhead and cut back most flowering shrubs as flowers fade
Midsummer	Potato sets for late crop	Carrots, chards, Chinese cabbages, kohl rabi, lettuces and salad crops, swedes, turnips and winter spinach	Incorporate compost with potato sets		Everything with diluted seaweed solution .... Maincrop potatoes with Bordeaux mixture in warm, humid weather	Evergreens and conifer hedges .... Deadhead regularly
Late summer	Daffodil bulbs	Japanese and spring onions, winter lettuces and salad crops, and winter spinach .... Green manures as soil becomes vacant			Everything with diluted seaweed solution	

Summary

Fruit	Routine tasks	In the greenhouse	Lawns and grass	Con-tainers	General	
Summer prune grapes Protect fruit from birds Thin, harvest and use ripening fruit	Weed regularly Water as required		Cut weekly		Check sticky bands Look for signs of pests (especially aphids, caterpillars, gooseberry sawflies and red spider mites) and diseases	Early summer
Prune plums and flowering and fruiting cherries Summer prune apple and pear trees Prune red- and white-currants and grape vines Protect fruit from birds Thin, harvest and use ripening fruit	Weed regularly Water as required		Cut as necessary Use clippings for mulch		Check sticky bands Looks for signs of pests and diseases Protect fruit from birds Put down water for birds	Midsummer
Cut out old blackcurrant stems after fruiting Transplant strawberry runners Protect fruit from birds Thin, harvest and use ripening fruit	Weed regularly Water as required		Cut as necessary Use clippings for mulch		Order hardy trees and shrubs for autumn planting Clean, paint and repair timber, gutters and brickwork Put down water for birds	Late summer

A year in the garden ~ Autumn

	Plant	Sow	Feed	Mulch	Spray	Prune
Early autumn	Garlic and other bulbs Transplant biennial flowering plants	Under cloches: Chinese greens, early carrots, turnips, winter lettuces and salad crops In the open: green manure	Incorporate compost with all transplants	Rake over old mulch	Everything with diluted seaweed solution	Herbaceous plants to 15cm (6in) as growth fades
Mid-autumn	Deciduous trees and shrubs	Sow summer cauliflowers and winter lettuces and salad crops; sweet peas; green manures	Incorporate compost with all plantings Spread sieved compost around trees, shrubs and soft fruit	Spread new mulch everywhere		Herbaceous plants to 15cm (6in) as growth fades Late-flowering shrubs as leaves fall
Late autumn	Deciduous shrubs and trees	Hardy broad beans and peas	Incorporate compost with all plantings Spread compost over asparagus and globe artichokes			Herbaceous plants to 15cm (6in) as growth fades Late-flowering shrubs as leaves fall

Autumn

Fruit	Routine tasks	In the greenhouse	Lawns and grass	Con-tainers	General	
Remove old raspberry and blackberry canes and tie in new ones Harvest and use or store	Weed regularly Lift and store dahlias and gladioli Take cuttings of woody plants before leaves drop		Cut as necessary Use clippings for mulch		Collect and store seed Check sticky bands Protect fruit and flowers from early frost Search for pests	**Early autumn**
Prune soft fruit and grape vines as the leaves fall Remove old raspberry and blackberry canes and tie in new ones Plant new soft fruit Harvest and use or store Put cloches over autumn strawberries	Weed regularly Lift and divide hardy herbaceous plants and rhubarb Make new beds and borders Put cloches over salad plants		Cut weekly, raising height of blade Leave clippings with shredded leaves or collect and use for mulch	Move indoors or under shelter	Collect and store seeds and berries Check sticky bands Protect borderline hardy plants against frost Turn compost heaps and cover Sieve well-rotted compost so it is ready for use	**Mid-autumn**
Winter prune apple, pears and non-stone fruit Plant soft fruit Harvest and store last fruit	Weed regularly In cold gardens lift and store root vegetables		Cut as necessary Collect clippings and use with leaves for mulch		Check sticky bands Order seed catalogues, potatoes and herbaceous plants for spring Collect waste for composting or shredding	**Late autumn**

A year in the garden ~ Winter

	Plant	Sow	Feed	Mulch	Spray	Prune
Early winter	Deciduous trees and shrubs		Incorporate compost with all plantings Spread compost over the crowns of herbaceous plants			Late-flowering shrubs as leaves fall
Midwinter	Chit potato seed in a light, frost-free place		Every few years spread lime or calcified seaweed over soil			Remove any damaged or diseased growth
Late winter	Garlic, onion sets and shallots Trees and shrubs		Spread seaweed on bare soil and mulches and rake in		Outdoor peaches and almonds with Bordeaux mixture	Remove any damaged or diseased growth

Fruit	Routine tasks	In the greenhouse	Lawns and grass	Containers	General	
Prune soft fruit and grape vines as leaves fall	Weed as necessary	Clean all glass and surfaces	Lime, aerate and spike, adding sharp sand, if needed		Check sticky bands	**Early winter**
Winter prune apples, pears and non-stone fruit	In mild gardens harvest and store root vegetables				Clean cloches and coldframes	
Plant soft fruit					Clean out gutters and drains when last leaves have fallen	
	Dig new beds				Plan and make changes	**Midwinter**
					Order seed	
					Put out food for birds	
Plant soft fruit	Set out cloches, low tunnels and sheet mulches to warm up soil	Sow broad beans, cabbages, carrots, cauliflowers, early peas, indoor tomatoes, lettuces, potatoes, radishes, spinach and turnips	Spread seaweed and rake in		Sieve and mix home-made potting compost	**Late winter**
Pick off big buds on blackcurrants			In mild weather cut with blade set high and leave clippings		Top up indoor beds with compost	
		In pots: onions and spring onions; sweet peas			Inspect ties, stakes and labels on woody plants	
					Firm roots of autumn planting after the last frosts	
					Check sticky bands	
					Empty insect traps and nests	

Index

Acknowledgements

All photography by Jerry Harpur except for the following listed below:
Bob Flowerdew back cover bottom
Garden Picture Library/David Cavagnaro 93
Holt Studios/Nigel Cattlin 28 left/Andy Morant 24
Leigh Jones 26
Octopus Publishing Group Limited 89 left/Mark Bolton 56/Michael Boyes 68/Dave Jordan front cover, back cover top/Peter Myers 28 right/George Wright 7, 80

Plant Illustrations **Susan Hillier**
Garden Plans **Cactus Design**

Editorial Manager **Jane Birch**
Executive Art Editor **Leigh Jones**
Designer **Peter Crump**
Picture Researcher **Jennifer Veall**
Production Controller **Lucy Woodhead**